SUBMISSION MADE EASY

A HANDBOOK FOR WOMEN AND MEN WHO CARE

A.E. OLAYEMI

O. A. ADEWOLE-BABATUNDE

SUBMISSION MADE EASY

A handbook for women and men who care

A.E. OLAYEMI

O. A. ADEWOLE-BABATUNDE

SUBMISSION MADE EASY

ISBN- 978-978-994-469-9

© 2021

Copyright © 2021 by

Abigail Ebun Olayemi,

Olubunmi Abiola Adewole-Babatunde

Published by:

FLORAL BLOOM NIGERIA LIMITED

For further information/Speaking

Engagement/Coaching

Please contact

+2348057420210

abiolababatunde0728@gmail.com,

olubunmispeakslife@gmail.com

Website: www.olubunmibabs.com

No portion of this publication maybe reproduced

without the written permission of the author.

ACKNOWLEDGEMENT

When the idea to write this book came in 2016, a lot was happening in my life. Candidly, I questioned the concept of submission even though I had embraced it. Talking with my mum (referred to as Abigail or Maami in this book) helped me. So, when I eventually stopped struggling and realized the strengths therein, I decided I wanted to write this book to honor her. The funny thing is, I discovered along the way that I still had lessons to learn. I am sure you too will be glad when you got to read her thoughts and not solely my interpretations of them.

Therefore, I will like to thank my mom (Abigail) for inspiring me to write this, teaching me most of the principles, showing me that they are doable and for always serving as a sounding board. I also want to thank my husband, Adewole Babatunde, for his love, support, and the gift of graceful leadership that made submission easy.

A big thank you to all the Olayemi and Babatunde family members. You are sources of joy and strength for me, and I cannot thank God enough for your lives. Thank you to all those who have allowed me and my mom to mentor and coach you through the years with these principles. Truthfully, we are honoured you will enable us to be your encouragers and scolders. God knows how grateful we are for you and how glad we are to see your marriages blessed.

Olubunmi Adewole-Babatunde (Mrs.)

<u>Dedication</u>

We dedicate this to all women who have considered building their homes and have worked tirelessly to achieve success. To women, who seem to have failed but are willing to get up and try again, we dedicate this to you. To all women seeking to build godly and happy homes, we are you and you are us. We share in your pains and glories, dear sisters.

To all men who have made submitting easy and graceful. To Prof Julius Yinka Olayemi, Abigail's husband and Olubunmi's Dad, an honorable, wise, loving, and conscientious man, we pray that you age gracefully Sir. To Dr. Adewole Babatunde, Olubunmi's husband, a gentle giant full of God's graceful meekness and strength, God honor you my dear son (Abigail speaking).

To the Lord who has been and continues to be our strength. Yes, to God, the Teacher of teachers, the Giver of Grace for submission in the school called marriage, we dedicate this book to You.

<u>ODE TO SUBMISSION</u>

We apologize to you, dear Submission

You have been sorely wronged

You have been attacked and called tyranny, abuse, docility, subservient and servitude

You have been suspected by both young and old

You have been accused of causing inferiority or demanding it of wives

You are ashamed of mindlessness, and yet people think it is your trademark

You hear men praise you for elements you are foreign to: acquiescence, lopsided relationships and a license to be self-centered

You have been stunned almost to a coma as society tries to strangle you out of the very homes where you would have saved the day and prevented chaos.

You are ashamed to be associated with some
movements that can only be called devilish and
abusive
But when you try to speak through those who know
you, they are sanctioned by mockery and disdain
Oh, how your accusers hate you. Can you still love
and live among us, dear Submission?

<u>Abigail and Olubunmi</u>

<u>TRIBUTE TO THE SUBMISSIVE WIFE</u>

For the devout women of the past who placed their hope in God used to make themselves beautiful by submitting themselves to their husbands. Sarah was like that; she obeyed Abraham and called him her master. You are now her daughter if you do good and are not afraid of anything. In the same way, you husbands must live with your wives with the proper understanding that they are more delicate than you. Treat them with respect because they also will receive, together with you, God's gift of life. Do this so that nothing will interfere with your prayers. (1 Peter 3:5-7, GNB)

She is calm, wise, resourceful, cheerful, full of confidence and courage. She knows her place, strengths, and weaknesses. She is a great negotiator and strategist. She is not fearful but chooses her Captain wisely. She understands her territory, knows how to create boundary lines while not always being guarded or insecure. She is full of love and life but knows just how to conserve and channel her much-valued energy. She is no pushover. She isn't a brain-dead doormat, nor is she some spineless bowl of jelly. She draws clear boundaries and humbly, yet gracefully enacts consequences if her husband becomes abusive. Her humble attitude remains intact even when saying "NO" or refusing to go along with sin. She is always willing to yield and let her king have the final vote but would pray her heart out to the Father above when she knows danger ensues in her husband's path.

She knows the power of words, cherishes her own words, and ensures that her words encourage, heal, love, accept, correct, inspire and communicate clearly. She is a woman of order and structure, and she has depth and insight; she has the foresight and maps a clear vision for her life and family. She is widely read and never myopic. Always ready to learn as she knows it makes her ever relevant. She knows that in her resides the heart and spirit, so when she is weak, her home risks chaos; when she is foolish, her home risks destruction.

She boldly, yet gently places the demands of honor, protection, wisdom and consideration on her Captain/Head/Husband. Demands are non-negotiable as they are her benchmark for co-operation even while they court and her heart is wooed. She knows where her loyalty lies. She knows she is a crucial player in her family's team structure. She submits willingly like Jesus, who had the power to drag equality with God but chose to bow to earn the greater good. She is no fool. She is not naïve or gullible but assured by her Creator that all surely would be well with Him playing the game of life with her. She knows that God has got her back and understands her.

She knows the role of the family in society. The family units make up the society, and she is determined to contribute positively to the community in her generation and for future generations.

She bears the title Matriarch of the family and proudly so. So, bring her crown, purchase the finest of

raiment because this woman is as fit as a Queen and
has proven her worth to sit right beside her King.
We doff our hats Submissive Woman

Abigail and Olubunmi

TABLE OF CONTENTS

17. Conclusion

On the third of January, 2012, I got out of a relationship. Having dealt with several emotionally draining situations, I was really tired of the whole marriage concept. I knew this was neither good news nor a good place to be, but I couldn't help myself. Two of my Pastors' wives and one of my paternal uncles spoke separately with me about this issue. May God bless them for doing so. As the year rolled by, I began to consider marriage again but then realized desperation was rising. Between June and December 2012, eleven men had either asked to marry me or have a serious relationship with me.

Don't worry, I wrote the number in words so that you wouldn't quickly notice it. Yes, I said 11. Self-awareness is priceless people: I realized that this was meant to scare me into either not making a decision or making a wrong one. A pastor of mine had counselled that in such situations women should realize that they are like a flower that has bloomed, has its seasons but wouldn't always continue to blossom. Hence a wise woman was not to take such a season of life for granted. She would be wise to calm down, make no hasty decisions and pay full attention. I knew I was in "trouble" because I was getting perplexed.

I asked God regarding all of them, and God didn't say anything. Stopping myself from acting in desperation was a battle in itself, but I found that joy allowed me to blow off the steam. It was a dark time. Other battles were raging from quarters that made no sense. I once visited a Pastor friend (of which I had many) whose husband is a Prophet. After catching up, her husband casually asked me about my relationships, and I opened up. He asked me to write out the names of all those asking for my hand in marriage, which I skeptically did because I was cautious of having someone else seeing or deciding who my spouse would be rather than receiving a word from God myself.

The list was only nine names (at the time). Upon looking through, he told me that my husband wasn't any of those on the list. He described my husband-his height, how he cut his beard, and his complexion. God knows I never thought of Wole (who is now my husband). (He and I were in a relationship several years before this, but I had opted out for reasons I will explain shortly). I had not seen him for six years, so I couldn't have known how he cut his beard. He also said that my husband will support me and will inspire me to be all that God intended. (This has been true in so many ways).

However, the Prophet also told me something was about to happen to confirm I would be married the following year. He told me a person very close to me would turn against me, and boy did that happen! The person brought rage, anger and utilized all the influence she could muster to attack. One day, while preaching at our church, she spent the 45minutes allotted to her to attack, insult, and incite people against me, or so it seemed. That day broke me. I remember walking to the back of the church, where I knelt down and prayed. I sensed that all that was happening was related to my marriage, so I knew this was time to surrender to God.

I knew I had been struggling and wanted to be in charge because I trusted myself more. The moment I told God I was willing to surrender totally, I asked Him who my spouse would be. He answered in less than 30 seconds that it was Wole. Note that Wole wasn't on the list of eleven men or the nine given to my friend's husband. I wasn't altogether thrilled, but I got what I needed. God answered because I had surrendered.

Oh yes, the Prophet was right. As soon as I could reach Wole, I asked for a recent picture. I was curious to know whether the description was as the man of God said. I was shocked it was just as he said. Who says there are no more true prophets! Funny enough, some five to six years earlier, my mom (who I fondly call Maami) had told me it was Wole she saw twice in her dream, but I did not submit to this idea. I was furious, and I told her it was because Wole was her Pastor's son back in Zaria. Thank God she took it calmly when I called her in my year of confusion. She merely said that she would pray for another revelation as she had put that episode behind her. That submission was something I found pretty difficult to do.

The lessons I learnt were enormous, and the one I need you to pay attention to here is that we only start the journey of grace in a marriage when we surrender to God. If you don't submit your will to God, you indeed won't submit to your spouse.

After submitting to God, I was glad and relieved but I also worried about His choice for me. The truth is that I had a specific picture in my head about who to marry, and my husband was so different. He was and is exceptionally gentle, which I thought was a weakness. Oh, silly me. God knew what was and is best for me. Yes, submitting to a peaceful and meek man is both easy and difficult, especially when your personality is boisterous and opinionated. When I tabled all my concerns before God, He answered swiftly that His grace is sufficient. That answer took me to research and study about grace like my life and future depended on it. It depends on it candidly. His grace has been truly sufficient, or do I say "more than sufficient". As Maami says: "submission begins first with God before agreeing to say 'Yes, I will.'"

THE HONOUR OF BIBLICAL SUBMISSION

"It is the disposition to follow a husband's authority and an inclination to yield to his leadership. It is an attitude that says, "I delight for you to take the initiative in our family. I am glad when you take responsibility for things and lead with love. I don't flourish when you are passive, and I have to make sure the family works." But the attitude of Christian submission also says, "It grieves me when you venture into sinful acts and want to take me with you. You know I can't do that. I have no desire to resist you. On the contrary, I flourish most when I can respond creatively and joyfully to your lead; but I can't follow you into sin, as much as I love to honor your leadership in our marriage. Christ is my King."

-------------John Piper

<u>Olubunmi's Years As A Young Child</u>

Growing up, I was the only biological daughter of my parents. I was close to my Mum for several reasons. First, I realized that I needed guidance. Secondly, I wanted sisters and didn't have any; so Mum had to play that role. We shared a common desire to have sisters though my mom's own was to have an elder sister, as is the first female-child of her parents. All her intimate friends as she grew up had elder sisters whom they called Aunty. This desire was one of the compelling reasons for agreeing to marry my father, according to her. My father had an elder brother, and Maami felt that the elder brother's wife would be what she lacked in her paternal home. He also had a younger sister who was older than her. So she felt she was going to have two Aunties in her married life.

I watched her go through several challenges in marriage. Initially, I was often infuriated and irritated at people who wouldn't treat her well. I promised myself I would not marry from my tribe. Thankfully Maami and I spoke a lot, and she was always willing to argue through my resistance and viewpoints. She and I were not on the same page for many years regarding Submission, but I realized the wisdom backing it up over time. Maami used to say, *"Stoop to conquer."* Yes, it is the title of a book but I wasn't willing to accept the principle.

This book that you are reading is birthed from the many arguments I had with Maami. I lost many of them as wisdom showed its preservative power over the years. Maami won on many grounds, and like I fondly tease her, she won as a Mafia Queen and Matriarch per excellence of the J.Y. Olayemi clan. My Dad most likely thinks he is the boss, but we the children know who rules with grace and such unassuming humility. You would boss her around and deceive yourself that you were in charge. I have also come to learn by experience in my own marriage the wisdom of submission.

While laying no claim to perfection, Maami and I decided to write this book to share wisdom and experiences for any couple, especially the wives, to learn early and keep their most treasured gift-their homes. We invite you to enjoy the counsel we share and hope that if you are a mother, you will share sound wisdom with your daughters or daughters-in-law to keep the family units together, thriving, and thus build a stable society.

Much love from us both.

-Abigail and Olubunmi

A WORD FROM OLUBUNMI'S HUSBAND

It's exciting to see the passion and energy that my wife has poured into this book on a topic that is controversial or that is thought to have patriarchal inclinations. With all sense of modesty, I think she has learnt and exhibited enough to be an advocate in this regard.

As she explained in this book, we had a break in our relationship before marriage because I was not exactly her typical definition of what her husband should be like. Being a boisterous, opinionated and strong-willed woman, she desired someone with similar or overriding charisma. That is easy to understand if you have met her brothers.

During our years apart, I had also ventured into different relationships and I refer to my experience in one to underscore the value of this book. My emotions during one of these relationships was one of feeling undermined, below myself and receiving of subtle and outright disrespect.

One striking difference that I noticed upon resuming my relationship with my wife was that I truly felt honoured. Truthfully, she had many societal reasons to be puffed up but the honour I received from her was simply awe-inspiring. Not only did she herself give the honour, she was also very protective that I did not receive dishonour from any quarters. And if you really want to see the fire in her eyes, then you would do something dishonouring to her husband. As I also got to learn, she came from a family that was big on honour and order.

Why would a strong-willed, opinionated, boisterous lawyer be willing to submit to a 'gentle', soft-spoken man? (I added her professional training because there is often a personality expected of lawyers). I guess she has already enumerated how she came to these conclusions in this book: first it is submission to God before submission to the man.

But what is the effect of this? Most men will agree that it is difficult not to love a woman that treats them with honour as compared with one that bruises their ego. When I look at these concepts, I can only submit to the wisdom of God in instructing married couples: 'Husbands love your wives, wives submit to your husbands'. It is easier for the husband to love a wife that submits to him. It is also easier for a wife to submit to a husband who loves her. Each of these speaks to a basic need of each gender: affection for women, respect for men.

None of this suggests being subservient as the authors explain. It also by no means suggests that the right of the wife is not protected. The Biblical principles provide a safety net in which the wife's heart is protected and the husband's honour is preserved. It is difficult to do one without the other, especially when we remember that these instructions end with 'as to the Lord' for wives and 'as Christ loved the church' for husbands (Ephesians 5:22 and 23). Therefore Christian marriage is not simply the husband and wife relating, but each of them relating with each other and to the Lord. So, yes, there is a third party to keep us all in check. And it is to Him that we ALL ultimately submit. (Ephesians 5:21)

Adewole Babatunde

CHAPTER 1.

<u>WHAT IS SUBMISSION?</u>

God knew what He was doing when He came up with the concept in Genesis 3:16

> *"And he said to the woman, "I will increase your trouble in pregnancy and your pain in giving birth. <u>In spite of this, you will still have the desire for your husband, yet you will be subject to him."</u> (GNT)*

Submission began on that dark day. We who have accepted Jesus as our Lord and Saviour are no longer under the Law or its curse. Galatians 3:13-14 puts it this way:

> *'"But by becoming a curse for us Christ has redeemed us from the curse that the Law brings; for the scripture says, "Anyone who is hanged on a tree is under God's curse." Christ did this so that the blessing God promised to Abraham might be given to*

the Gentiles through Christ Jesus so that through faith, we might receive the Spirit promised by God.' (GNT)

As God sees it, submission creates order in any system. Take a look at how the hierarchy is spelled out.

Wives, submit yourselves to your husbands as to the Lord. For a husband has authority over his wife just as Christ has control over the church, and Christ is himself the Saviour of the church, his body[1]. And so wives must submit themselves entirely to their husbands just as the church submits itself to Christ. Husbands, love your wives just as Christ loved the church and gave His life for it. He did this to dedicate the church to God by his word, after making it clean by washing it in water, to present the church to Himself in all its beauty—pure and faultless, without spot or wrinkle or any other imperfection.

> *Men ought to love their wives just as they love their bodies. A man who loves his wife loves himself. (None of us ever hate our bodies. Instead, we feed them and take care of them, just as Christ does the*

church, for we are members of His body. As the scripture says, "For this reason, a man will leave his father and mother and unite with his wife, and the two will become one." This scripture reveals a profound secret truth, which I understand applies to Christ and the church. But it also applies to you: every husband must love his wife as himself, and every wife must respect her husband. Ephesians 5:22-33 (GNT)

In the family, we all answer to God in this order: JESUS ANSWERS TO THE FATHER, THE HUSBAND TO JESUS, and <u>THE WIFE TO THE HUSBAND.</u>

Submission is *the state of being wholly controlled or keeping* oneself under the authority of another person or a group and agreeing to obey them. Submission calls for a level of understanding of the "authority" regarding the authority's roles, responsibilities, limitations, capabilities, strengths, and weaknesses. Understanding who one is to submit to is a prudent approach to submission. Many setups in life require the concept of submission, but marriage tops the list. The widely accepted, though controversial, mindset is that the wife submits. This is true and, at the same time, false. Submission is simply being considerate of the other person while deciding or making plans, so a wise man would submit to his wife along the way and daily. *Ephesians 5:21 (NLT)- And further, submit to one another out of reverence for Christ.*

Submission is the act of someone who acknowledges legitimate authority and willingly comports themselves accordingly. It has to be voluntary. It is not forced. Otherwise, it becomes subservience. In military terminology, it is the ability to arrange military troop divisions under the command of a leader.

Submission can also be seen as a woman's happy response to her husband's biblical leadership or headship. An intelligent, happy, and wise support for your husband's leadership means a lot to him. It is the calling of a wife to honor and affirm her husband's leadership and help carry it through according to her gifts. Leadership is not superior competency. It is boldness or courage to take the initiative, be responsible and face challenges. Submission is a mindful, joyful, willing, intelligent, loving cooperation to a husband's God-ordained position as the head of the home.

> *'Wives, submit yourselves to your husbands as to the Lord. For a husband has authority over his wife just as Christ has authority over the church; and Christ is himself the Saviour of the church, his body. And so wives must submit themselves completely to their husbands just as the church submits itself to Christ.'*
> *Ephesians 5:22-24* (GNT)

Submission begins with the "yes" answer to "Would you marry me?" The word "completely" often sends shivers down the spine of many women. You might ask whether there are areas in which they don't want their husbands involved or situations in which they would not wish to submit to him? I subscribe to submitting all areas of your life to your spouse. Olubunmi once told me that during a sisters' fellowship held during her service year in Zamfara, she accepted the idea of submitting her life's earnings since she was willing to surrender her body to her husband. What is more significant than her body? Nothing, not even finances.

However, I think most women grapple more with submitting in all situations. Of course, the general rule is that you submit in all conditions **except** where evil, sin, or illegal activities arise. Consider the story of Ananias and Sapphira:

> *But there was a man named Ananias, who with his wife Sapphira sold some property that belonged to them. But with his wife's agreement, he kept part of the money for himself and turned the rest over to the apostles. Peter said to him, "Ananias, why did you let Satan take control of you and make you lie to the Holy Spirit by keeping part of the money you received for the property? Before you sold the property, it belonged to you; and after you sold it, the money was yours. Why, then, did you decide to do such a thing? You have not lied to people—you have lied to God!"*

As soon as Ananias heard this, he fell dead; and all who heard about it were terrified. The young men came in, wrapped up his body, carried him out, and buried him. About three hours later his wife, not knowing what had happened, came in. Peter asked her, "Tell me, was this the full amount you and your husband received for your property?" "Yes," she answered, "the full amount."

So Peter said to her, "Why did you and your husband decide to put the Lord's Spirit to the test? The men who buried your husband are at the door right now, and they will carry you out too!" At once, she fell at his feet and died. The young men came in and saw that she was dead, so they carried her out and buried her beside her husband. The whole church and all the others who heard of this were terrified. Act 5:1-11 (GNT)

The story of Peter and John also teaches the same principle:

So they called them back in and told them that under no condition were they to speak or teach in the name of Jesus. But Peter and John answered them, "You

Some wives need to save themselves with wisdom where necessary. Do you remember the story of Abigail and Nabal? Their lives would have been wasted due to David's wrath but for the timely intervention of Abigail. Remember, her action was not in accord or obedient to her husband's wishes as he refused to give David's troops food and drinks but she went ahead and saved lives. *See 1 Samuel 25:2-35.*

What should one do if asked by the husband to do what is evil, sinful, or offensive? Speak up calmly and respectfully. Your prayer life is paramount here. You can still submit by not being the one to report him or creating a scene, but you must avoid falling into sin with him if he has chosen to walk that path. Your calm and respectful attitude, devoid of arrogance, will significantly serve you here. If he repents, great news.

If he doesn't, at least you did not perish with him and leave your children to suffer alone. We all answer first to God and then to physical authorities over us. A man who won't submit to God should still be submitted to but in a manner that pleases God. Consider this:

"In the same way you wives must submit yourselves to your husbands so that if any of them do not believe God's word, your conduct will win them over to believe. It will not be necessary for you to say a word because they will see how pure and reverent your conduct is". 1 Peter 3:1-2 (GNT)

You must realize that each party in a marriage is a valuable player. Each person brings a unique selling point or value proposition. Our abilities and viewpoints differ, and when each realizes this and recognizes them as advantages and not threats, it helps to adopt an inclusivity approach.

> *In the same way, you wives must submit yourselves to your husbands so that if any of them do not believe God's word, your conduct will win them over to believe. It will not be necessary for you to say a*

word because they will see how pure and reverent your conduct is.

You should not use outward aids to make yourselves beautiful, such as the way you fix your hair, or the jewelry you put on, or the dresses you wear. Instead, your beauty should consist of your true inner self, the ageless beauty of a gentle and quiet spirit, which is of the greatest value in God's sight. The devout women of the past who placed their hope in God used to make themselves beautiful by submitting themselves to their husbands.

Sarah was like that; she obeyed Abraham and called him her master. You are now her daughter if you do good and are not afraid of anything. In the same way, your husbands must live with your wives with the proper understanding that they are more delicate than you. Treat them with respect, because they also will receive, together with you, God's gift of life. Do this so that nothing will interfere with your prayers. 1 Peter 3:1-7 (GNT)

Love must be completely sincere. Hate what is evil, hold on to what is good. 10 Love one another warmly as Christians, and be eager to show respect for one another. Romans 12:9-10 (GNT)

A point of view that we women must gain is that a submissive wife is a respected armor-bearer. In the Old Testament, kings selected certain officers to stand with them in war and bear their armor. You might want to read the following passage that refers to armor bearers in the Bible:

"Do what you think is best," the armor-bearer replied. "I'm with you completely, whatever you decide." I Samuel 14:7 (NLT)

An armor bearer is a soldier (usually a senior officer) to who a King is willing to entrust his life and most-priced tools of war. His means of warfare symbolize tools he uses for fulfilling purposes, protecting his territory, and self-preservation. An armor bearer serves in several capacities, and no one else should play this role in a marriage other than the wife. So if being called a submissive wife bothers you (in any case, that is a problem), consider yourself your husband's armor-bearer. Take a look at what an armor bearer does:

Qualities of a True Armor bearer[2]

· Awakens and arouses his leader, helping him to stand against all foes.

· Carries and handles his leader's weapons resourcefully.

· Moves quickly alongside his leader through the thick of battle as a forceful escort who never falls behind.

· Protects and watches out for his leader continually and continuously.

· Repels any type of attack against his leader.

· Rescues his leader from all difficulties and hardships.

· Moves to completely resist every enemy advance that comes against his leader to do him harm.

· Opposes and routs his leader's enemies swiftly and forcefully.

---

[2] Qualities of an Armorbearer - cfaith. https://www.cfaith.com/index.php/blog/22-articles/christian-living/19833-qualities-of-an-armorbearer?tmpl=component Accessed 26th June, 2021

· Remains always on duty at his leader's side to tend to any need.

· Keeps one eye on the leader at all times and the other eye trained on the enemy, anticipating both actions.

· Surrenders completely to his leader, trusting him implicitly and obeying without hesitation

· Carries out every plan of his leader successfully.

· Completes his leader's commands perfectly.

· Assists his leader in all activities and undertakings.

· Organizes and arranges his leader's activities.

· Prepares and cares for his leader's belongings.

· Takes very special care in selecting and preparing his leader's supplies.

· Anticipates his leader's needs and demands to furnish and supply what is appropriately needed.

· Keeps his eye on the road ahead to point out any danger or pitfall to his leader.

· Recognizes and brings any questionable matters or vital information to his leader.

· Strives to make his leader's surroundings more pleasant and bearable.

· Develops an eye for detail.

· Helps bring an acceleration in growth and promotion to his leader's progress.

· Places emphasize enhancing the leader's position, guarding against personal jealousy, envy, or selfishness.

· Exalts, respects, and uplifts his leader at all times.

· Watches for his officer's every reward, claiming those that the leader may have overlooked.

· Works tirelessly and diligently on behalf of his leader, seeking ways to advance his welfare and situation.

· Fulfils his leader in every way, getting along with him and making him feel comfortable giving orders.

· Sacrifices his own life and well-being for the betterment of his leader.

· Works for his leader's welfare at all times.

· Demonstrates total intolerance of any false charge made against his leader.

· Shares the dreams, goals, and visions of his leader.

· Desires to see his leader "get ahead." He immediately forgives his leader for any offense without harboring resentment or anger.

· Refuses to hold a grudge against his leader for any reason.

· Demonstrates extreme loyalty to his leader, even unto death.

· Completes and complements his leader.

· Flows well with his leader.

· Esteems his leader as more important than himself.

It is evident by now that a biblical armor-bearer was much more than just a hired hand. An armor-bearer was a person who undoubtedly spent many years, if not his entire life, in the king's service. Only in this manner could he come to know and understand the king.

Have you read through this list? Who else is equipped and available to play these roles in your marriage for your husband? If you can offer another name besides yourself, you are most likely creating a gap in your home. The devil will seek out who would steal that space from you, so be mindful.

CHAPTER 2.

WHY THE CONCEPT OF SUBMISSION?

Submission, as a concept, is not unique to marriage. You would find situations and instructions in the Bible about a younger person submitting to the older, the Church to Christ Jesus, Christ Jesus to God the Father, children to parents, a husband to his wife, believers to God, people to the government, church members to church leadership, believers to other believers, Jesus to his earthly parents and of course, servants to bosses. See *Philippians 2:5-11, Hebrews 12:9, James 4: 7, Ephesians 5:21-24, Colossians 1:18, Hebrews 13:17, Romans 13:1-7, Mark 12:17, Titus 3:1, 1 Peter 2:13-14, Ephesians 6:1-8, 1 Peter 5:5, Ephesians 5: 25-33.*

The concept is everywhere in life, so I am surprised that it is vehemently attacked in marriage. In civil service, remember that when a junior staff misbehaves, he is often cited for insubordination. Submission is alive and well even in a sports team, social clubs, business places, etc. So why is it hated so much in marriage? I know that it is often because of records and experiences of abuse. At other times, it's the devil manipulating things and causing strife because he knows the premium and value of marriage in society and the church.

The Attack on Submission

It has become so bad that in some circles if a woman were to state that she is under authority, people would hope she means that she is being abused or that she is speaking of her Father or boss at work. They frown if they hear it is her husband. There is always an authority figure in every setup where human beings exist. Even among children, they choose a class captain and learn to follow his or her lead. Should the same democratic approach to determining who should head the home be adopted? No, because God didn't think so in His sovereign wisdom. He chose the man, the husband, to lead.

Ladies who wrestle with the concept of marriage must distinguish between their valid fear of oppression in the general world (such as their workplace) and their fear of intimidation in marriage. In marriage, just as in the world, oppression and dominance are unacceptable, but this doesn't make revolting against submission acceptable. In the general world, feminism summarizes the fight not to demean, maltreat, marginalize, or abuse women but to give them equal space in life. I (Olubunmi) am a feminist myself. Still, I would first scream that the scope of feminism must be defined not to infiltrate our homes and marriages. In Biblical marriage, we are equal before God-

> *"It is through faith that all of you are God's children in union with Christ Jesus. You were baptized into union with Christ, and now you are clothed, so to speak, with the life of Christ himself. So there is no difference between Jews and Gentiles, between*

slaves and free people, between men and women; you are all one in union with Christ Jesus. If you belong to Christ, then you are the descendants of Abraham and will receive what God has promised."
Galatians 3:226-29 (GNT)

Our equality is never to be debated, forming the basis of mutual respect and honor. Submission in marriage asks for the ability to step back, hold on, and be meek enough to allow the husband to lead.

The Need For Submission

See, I (Olubunmi) love movies, so let's act a few.

Scenario 1-

Imagine having an emergency where you have cut your hand, and the bleeding is profound. You rush into the hospital, and while you groan in pain and see your blood paint the floor, you hear the nurse arguing with the doctor about what to do. You hear the nurse shout that the doctor is demeaning her by asking her to clean your wound. The doctor then caves in, so you don't bleed to death; he cleans your wound and turns to the nurse for further instructions. What would be running through your mind? Is the nurse valuable and vital? Yes, oh yes. But while she might have lots of experience, maybe because she has been in practice for five years and the doctor for only six months, the drama probably wouldn't sit well in your mind- this is the value of submission to authority. The nurse should have submitted.

Scenario 2-

Imagine that you are on a flight heading from Nigeria to Norway for a scholarship Master's program. You are excited that your life is taking a different turn - the higher level, you might think. During the flight, you realize it got turbulent. You are worried and curious; you want to know why? You recognize that the weather seems good. People with you on the flight know it's not the weather. Then you hear an argument that shocks you out of your wits. It's from the cockpit. The two pilots are arguing about how to proceed on the trip. In your innocent but worried mind, you are asking who is senior. Shouldn't the junior submit to the senior?

You don't understand what they are saying, and you don't care. You want order, you want peace, and you want to get to your destination in one piece. Even if the senior is barking orders, you don't care; the junior should be humble enough to handle that later when lives aren't at risk. There has to be some disciplinary or conflict resolution measures to address their concerns, but you are sure that now isn't the best time for that. This is the submission's value and place.

Scenario 3-

You are on a cruise with your family. You have all the activities planned out. You have planned and prepared for this for years. Your hopes of rekindling your love with your husband are high. You know that this is what you need. On day three of the eight-day trip, you hear an alarm asking passengers to wear their life jackets and get into the available lifeboats as the ship might sink if it hits an iceberg in its direction. That confuses you because you wonder why the boat can't be redirected from the iceberg. But you think you should obey. You run to your family like death is chasing you.

Then you hear another announcement. This time, a different voice says you should remain calm and jettison the previous instructions. You are now panicked and disoriented. Your husband is as confused as you are. You both ask some of the staff, and they tell you the first announcement was by the junior Captain and the second by his senior. You ask why the announcements were different and why the junior even made any announcement, as you know it wasn't his place to make it. You start to make calls all over the world. You and your husband are arguing about what to do. Some passengers are already heeding the first instructions. You don't know what to do. You are terrified this might be another Titanic, and you might not live to tell the story. You are annoyed at both Captains and want to get to safety physically and emotionally. Your children are all worried and scared.

Because the Senior Captain comes to reassure you all, and you all feel the ship turn forcefully, you realize the threat to the ship is gone. You can now breathe easily. Days four through eight are more of you and your family counting down and enduring the voyage. You notice that people are restless and nervous no matter how much fun or entertaining activities the ship's crew offer. The experience was traumatic. You and your husband tell yourselves- **NEVER AGAIN**, and when it ends, you bid the ship farewell.

You know where the submission angle is. Insubordination is what the junior Captain would be accused of and disciplined for. Yet, while you empathize with him and understand that he wanted to save lives (yours inclusive), you wish his approach differed. You would have liked to know (I imagine) that both Captains were in sync, conversed, weighed the options, and reached a conclusion or that, in a worst-case scenario, the junior submitted to the authority of the senior.

Scenario 4-

You are King David in Bible times. You have a busy day that consists of battles with nations around you. Sadly, internal family issues are also on your plate, like one of your sons desperately seeking to kill you. You know that he has infiltrated trusted officers. Some of the wives you foolishly acquired are fighting because they all know the story that led to this. Your weaknesses stare you in the face, and you can't seem to find assistance but in God. Then you remember that you still have some loyal, experienced, trusted officers with you, and your Armor bearer is top on your list. You know the only order or instruction he will never obey from you is one to commit a sin or to harm you. The value of an armor bearer is unquantifiable. You, the wife, are that armor bearer in your marriage, giving your husband the confidence to fight and win his life battles.

I know that marriage relationships always generate far more fracas. The world sees women as victims ab initio. The world can't be blamed because many men intimidate, abuse, and harm their spouses than protect, love, and honor them. While the problems are real, one had better separate the issues.

A woman who submits does not do it because it's an ugly demand on her. God expects and instructs her to submit. She maintains love, unity, and order and knows how and when to voice her priceless opinions. An abusive man is not to be punished with a lack of submission. He should be corrected for lack of obedience to God's instructions. He should be treated with love. The wife must be graceful and wise enough to protect herself. If a husband beats his wife, she should find help and protection to prevent recurrence right after surviving the first experience. There are several legal redresses and safety approaches. It must be utilized (even temporarily) if physically getting away can be done. No woman is expected under God to return to a violent home. God hates violence. *I Timothy 3:3, Isaiah 60:18, Proverbs 3:31.*

> **"The Lord examines both the righteous and the wicked. He hates those who love violence". Psalm 11:5 (NLT)**

"And I will require the blood of anyone who takes another person's life. If a wild animal kills a person, it must die. And anyone who murders a fellow human must die. If anyone takes a human life, that person's life will also be taken by human hands. For God made human beings in his own image." Genesis 9:5-6 (NLT)

Submission in marriage might not be familiar to some women for various reasons. Consider the following:

a. the lady grew up seeing her mother being abused and forced to submit,

b. a single mum raised her, and some men did not treat her mum right

c. a mum, though married, was the head of the home

d. a lady who embraces the extreme of the feminist movement even in marriage

e. she has been influenced by the media, which tends to mock and criticize godly principles.

There is a likelihood that a woman in any of these categories would find the concept of submission as the enemy she must resist. She may not see any value or good in it.

True freedom is living under well-defined and loving authority. There is safety in God-ordained authority structures, and there is a need for a godly balance between liberty and accepting authority. The design of the home and marriage includes the pillar of submission. Submission as a pillar of a home is a crucial structural item. Chaos is never far from where no one is submitting, so the order is lost, and trouble brews daily.

The concept of submission is essential, and it is a wise approach to ensure that undue power play does not lead to the fracturing of a marriage. The most basic foundation of submission is mutual respect for the will and the uniqueness of the person to whom one is married. When submission is understood, accepted, and utilized rightly, the following are sure to occur:

1. The couple has a higher chance of exercising Christian authority over darkness.

2. They would learn the benefits of having boundaries in life.

3. The quality of their relationship would improve.

4. They both could relate to authority figures and structures with greater ease.

5. They would show their children godly approaches to marriage and life in general.

6. They and their children would grow to manage conflict well.

7. They would learn to better discern God's design of order in marriage.

8. They will build healthy and well-rounded children, which God desires (Malachi 2:15).

9. They will have a better understanding of God's design for leadership.

Some men are arrogant about their role as a leader in the family. Arrogance is risky and fails to follow Jesus' example. Some men have been shamed into shying away from the authority position in their homes. Some women cringe at mentioning the word authority with their husbands' names. Many may be responsible: for disappointments about past poor behaviors from their husband, outright disrespect of him, the influence of society, and much more.

Every woman needs to understand that every man would disappoint or fail at something or at some time. They are human, just like we are. This is where being forgiving and compassionate is helpful. Also, if you disrespect him for whatever reason, you would be wise to deal with it in your heart. It is one thing to protect oneself from abuse by him and another to live a life of disrespect towards him. Disrespect from a wife to her husband is a form of emotional abuse and the brewing of offense on her part.

I have observed that when women attack the concept of submission, their displeasure with the idea of authority is right behind them. Undoubtedly, there are poor examples of authority figures (even husbands). Still, the way to handle it is not to lead a revolution in the home. Would your children be doing right if you as parents disappoint them, and they overthrow you to play the parents' role?

One must deal decisively and tactfully with the wrong behaviors the authority figure (husband) brings to the home. If it is laxity, irresponsibility, abuse, etc., search for the wise approach to handling it. Even if you must leave the house (which is advisable if he is physically abusive), try your best not to be disrespectful. Your safety is the focus, and not getting back at him. Allow the Law to deal with him by reporting the abuse, but don't attempt to harm him, which the Law would need to hold you accountable for.

CHAPTER 3.

<u>WHY SHOULD A WIFE SUBMIT?</u>

Olubunmi and I are women are women, so it may not suffice for us to slam the "it is Biblical" card on you and leave you at that. God has His reasons for inspiring the strategy, so that is the viewpoint I (Abigail) would share with you. Olubunmi struggled with it, and truthfully, it is not altogether easy, especially if you don't believe in or subscribe to the concept.

The older generation didn't know any different, so we did not fight the concept. We probably saw it as humility, plus a lot of loyalty, and hoped we would someday be called good wives by our in-laws and husbands. Nevertheless, having a good understanding of a concept is always better.

Now, obeying an instruction from God's Word is wisdom and very beneficial. Obedience comes with its blessings. The thoughts that I intend to share with you are additional considerations that would help, and hopefully assist, you in deciding to give your heart and intellect to the concept of submission in your marriage.

First, my consolation is that when I submit, the person who takes the heat is my husband, not me. People know when you are submitting; they see the structure of your home from the outside. Sometimes, when a woman is accused of not being submissive or is ruling in her house by control, manipulation, or force, people see that as well. Then you might have attacks from different quarters, and you, as the wife, are asked to answer for actions and decisions you should not have been asked to account for. With submission, one enjoys cover and peace. Tony Evans puts it wittily and with humour when he said:

"Spiritual headship is God telling the woman to duck so he can punch the man."

A man is meant to be the covering for his wife and children. The wife stays under her husband's "covering" through submission. Some of us women are very irritated by our husband's way of covering, probably because some of them are (to us) clueless. The way to rectify that is to pray for and with him, lovingly encourage him through books, materials, talks, programs, and godly relationships such as mentorship, and not by shaming him or taking the lead from him. Try seeing things from his perspective. Communicate, talk, and discuss with him. Some wives don't appreciate this concept of covering. Imagine how a widow or a fatherless child feels. So, don't diminish your husband's role as head, protector, and cover.

A woman's delicate role in marriage requires being shielded from undue combat because she is the heart of the home. Continually faced with strife or the burden of being the frontline leader is not God's design, and candidly, women were not fashioned for such a setup.

Second is the fact that the children are observing. Just like Olubunmi watched me (her Mum) for years and went through the mental accent and rejection several times, your children are observing and asking whether it is possible to keep things together in a marriage or whether strife is the way forward.

Another reason is that it is wisdom in disguise. Have you ever imagined being on a ship? Somebody tells you there are two qualified and experienced captains who never agree on anything? Just imagine how you would feel. Their certifications and years of experience would not console you. They must work as a team to get you and all other passengers to the shore. Submission is the compelling agreement one of such captains has to offer to keep everyone safe. Yes, both parties in a marriage must learn to submit one to another just as *Ephesians 5:21* demands but the wife primarily as *Ephesians 5:24* states.

Find it in your heart as a wife to put yourself under your husband's authority. You still have a say and can influence things behind the scene but without the exposure of the responsibility of taking the hit or the blame if ever things or situations are challenged.

Many who have experienced widowhood have expressed how exposing and tedious it is to be the head of the home and face all the challenges without a man's cover. A husband is not only a provider but also a protector. Many cultures respect men so much that their presence in the home sets a standard and a warning to all reckless or disrespectful minds to stay clear or answer to the man of the house. I (Olubunmi) am married to the most gentle and calm man I have ever met. Still, even at that, some people are mindful of his presence in my life and desist from harassing me. Allow your husband to protect you. I have described it as staying under his canopy. I joke that it might seem as small as an umbrella sometimes, but I must find its scope and stay under it.

I (Abigail) have counselled several women and found that their vocal thoughts are the number one way to get outside the scope of their spouse's cover. The world thinks that being an independent woman means voicing every opinion, being a feminist, and being bold with every view. This could end up being foolish. This is not to subscribe to fear but to be reminded that wisdom is motivated by preservation principles. Many wars have been ignited by statements made by men leading governments through the years. Some were mere threats, yet led to outright massacres. Words have power, as *James 3:6* reveals. Your opinions need not always be shared. I (Olubunmi) am a strongly opinionated woman and, most of the time, believe in the efficacy of my views. Still, I am wise enough to know the thoughts to share, when, who to share them with, or whether or not to share them. Realize that in life, you make friends and enemies. It is wise to be prudent. Who wants enemies close to home? Be guided by these straightforward questions-

- Is it worth it?
- What is it that I want to say?
- Where do I want to say it?
- When do I want to say it?
- To whom do I want to say it?

- Why do I want to say it?

- What do I gain by saying it?

- Would the person hearing it misquote me somewhere else?

- Would I be glad repeating this somewhere else?

Some years ago, a woman made accusations against her husband just to hurt him. In her words, it was revenge because she felt she could scare him. She knew the allegations were false but desperately wanted to mar his name. She succeeded in her mission but made so many enemies and showed the world that she was not under his cover and had no regard for him. I can only imagine the number of storms she alone would need to calm down because of the mess she created. Silence is golden, many at times.

Please realize that you can choose whether or not to be covered. Believe it or not, it is dangerous not to be covered. You can expose yourself and decide to be the boss. Men often choose one of two options when a woman leads the family. They either sit back and wait for things to blow up (and are quick to show

how their wife frustrated their efforts to lead), or they go rogue, where they fight tooth and nail for dominance and might hurt the wife in the process. You might likely not enjoy the outcome either way. Hence it is essential to be wise and choose to submit in a graceful yet intelligent manner so that you can still negotiate the scope and operation of the submission in your marriage.

CHAPTER 4.

<u>WHAT SUBMISSION IS</u>

<u>NOT</u>

This chapter will examine why women hate the concept of submission. For many, it starts as early as when growing up. Many people, including men, do not realize that many misunderstood interpretations make it undesirable. Who wants to be in a straitjacket? Who wants to feel limited or treated as inconsequential? Many men who bully their wives do not want their daughters to taste a fraction of what they put their wives through. The concerns are real. Below is a list of what submission is not; check them out. Are they real to you or not?

1. Submission is not allowing the man to make decisions unilaterally. Communication is a

two-way thing that every healthy marriage utilizes.

2. It is not meant to guide or goad you into sin, crime, or evil.

3. It is not where a spouse simply agrees to everything without considering it. Consequences are real, and what affects one party in a marriage would involve both parties in the long run.

4. Submission does not mean agreeing with everything your husband says.

5. It does not mean living or acting in fear.

6. Submission does not mean you do not try to influence your husband positively[3]. Do not derelict in your duties. Suppose your husband is falling away or attempting to tread a destructive path, in that case, you are responsible for lovingly correcting, warning, praying for him, and encouraging him in the right direction. Therefore, don't excuse yourself

---

[3] Six Things Submission Is Not | Desiring God.
https://www.desiringgod.org/articles/six-things-submission-is-not

and claim it was you submitting. Remember what the Bible says: *In the same way, you wives must submit yourselves to your husbands so that if any of them do not believe God's word, your conduct will win them over to believe. It will not be necessary for you to say a word.* **1Peter 3:1** (GNT)

7. Submission does not mean a wife gets her personal, spiritual strength from her husband.[4]

8. Submission does not mean avoiding trying to change a husband and yourself for good.

9. Submission does not mean leaving your brain or your will at the wedding altar.[5]

10. It does not mean the husband is always right, and neither are you.

11. Submission does not mean putting your husband's will before Christ's will.

12. It is not a license to be abusive or become a bully.

---

[4] Six Things Submission Is Not | Desiring God.
https://www.desiringgod.org/articles/six-things-submission-is-not
[5] What Biblical Submission Does and Does Not Mean.
https://www.thegospelcoalition.org/blogs/justin-taylor/what-biblical-submission-does-and-does/

Chapter 5.

THE ELEMENTS OF SUBMISSION

It Starts with Submission to God

Remember my (Olubunmi's) story at the start of this book? Submission in marriage is practically impossible where a woman has refused to submit to God. See *Luke 1:26-38. Verse 38 records Mary's words: "I am the Lord's servant," said Mary; "may it happen to me as you have said." And the angel left her.* (GNT) It all starts at God's feet. Jesus prayed a prayer that is worth paying attention to. These were His words- **Luke 22:42, "Father," he said, "if you will take this cup of suffering away from me. Not my will, however, but your will be done."** (GNT) And after that, in verse 43 of the same Chapter, an angel from heaven appeared to him and strengthened him.

Did you notice how similar both their statements are? It was a progression; first, they acknowledged God's infinite power and eternal nature. Then they surrendered to His will and finally received strength for the challenges. Yes, sadly, challenges do come in life. If you don't submit, do not expect grace and enablement for the journey. Grace would just not come because you do not dictate the destiny assignments you were crafted for.

So, if you don't submit to God, you cannot adequately submit to your husband. The truth is that we serve and love our families as service unto God and not excluding Him. It is never only about pleasing the husband or making the lives of your family members peaceful. It's a journey that starts with God. After I surrendered to Him, He answered my question about who my spouse was.

Start the journey with God.

I have noticed that there are two elements of submission. These are the internal and external elements of submission. Internal factors are those you can control, influence, or improve upon if you choose to:

1. **A humble heart.** Everyone must instruct their heart. Pride and arrogance are a choice and can be avoided simply by adopting modest approaches to life—simple things like courtesies, apologies, and regard for others' help.

2. **A Secure heart.** Insecurity can make a person anxious and unstable. People who feel insecure do not allow others to protect them and hardly trust others. They often try to remain in control or manipulate things to go their way. Working on one's insecurities can help rest and allow the husband to lead without much worry or combat.

3. **Heart of wisdom.** Wisdom is gained consciously and by God's intervention if one asks for it. It is essential to be wise. Wisdom is simply the proper use of information gathered and understood. It may simply be called strategy.

4. **Meekness.** This is the ability to control your reactions, abilities, and words. The ability to control is not automatic. Everyone learns daily, and sometimes, due to bad experiences, one learns faster. A meek woman knows her rights. She is not a fool or fearful. Still, she is so aware of the power of her actions and the possible consequences that she weighs them well before dishing out words or actions.

5. **Trust in God** -even when situations are difficult. The Lord can turn the water of an ordinary marriage into the wine of an enriched one. The miracle-working God sprang that surprise at Cana of Galilee. John 2:1-25. Invite Him, obey Him. Tell Him your shortcomings and follow His instructions.

6. **She knows there is no perfect husband or wife.** We are all flawed human beings; therefore, she quickly forgives.

7. **Eyes fixed on Jesus.** Jesus must be our focus of attention because there will always be new philosophies and arguments. Only His words

can be fulfilling when we hear, "Well done, good and faithful servant!..."

External elements (as you must have figured out) aren't within your control but give you a viewpoint of what you are up against. They are vital pieces of information you must give attention to:

1. **Antecedents:** What is your spouse's (or spouses-to-be) antecedents? If you know your spouse-to-be is hot-tempered, a bully, manipulative, or controlling, you are toying with trouble by uniting in marriage with him because you must submit in marriage. We don't get to choose whether to submit to only their strengths.

2. **His Submission to God:** Is your spouse (or spouses-to-be) submissive to God? The best-case scenario is that we all learn to submit to superior authorities. Like in the case of a ladder, one bar is accountable/responsible to the other, on and on till the peak. All these speak to accountability. If your spouse is accountable

and willing to be responsible to God, in particular, you are safe to a large extent.

3. **His Love for God:** Does your spouse (or spouse-to-be) love God? Loving God and serving Him are two different things. Love inspires service, but fear also motivates service. Hence, the better situation is a passionate love for God and a healthy dose of fear and reverence for God. This serves as a check and guides one's decision-making and conduct, primarily where a wife cannot compel her spouse.

4. **His Accountability to Others:** Is your spouse (or spouse-to-be) accountable to any other human being? Some people (both male and female) do not have anyone who can call them to order when they misbehave or act foolishly. You might say you respect your spouse. Great, but who else? You and your spouse need to be able to submit to the authority of another human being. Such a person had better have values that inspire you to be better and godlier.

Making a conscious effort to make such connections is paramount and can save a marriage if crises occur. My husband and I (Olubunmi) are answerable to a couple we approached formally for discipleship or mentorship. My husband also has several people he respects and would listen to if the need arises. I love that he has excellent/godly friends and respects his elder brother. He also knows that I answer to my parents and one of my brothers as a spiritual head besides other pastors I respect and listen to.

CHAPTER 6.

<u>TEAMWORK IN MARRIAGE</u>

One of the most vital tools for enjoying peace in marriage is teamwork. Taking pressure off one another should be your mutual desire. It can be achieved by supporting each other. There is a need for synergy and coordination if a marriage would be peaceful and productive on all fronts. As such, some mindsets would greatly help. Some of these are as follows:

1. **Anti-stereotypic Viewpoint.** Every culture has its traditions and practices. This may pose a challenge, especially in cross-cultural marriages. However, where the couple is willing to vary and adapt would assist in creating a team,

mainly as they now constitute a new culture in Christ. The focus is on the desired outcome.

This may contradict a stereotypic idea that only a particular person should do a specific thing. For instance, in many cultures, a woman is widely expected to run the domestic affairs of the house. Most women would agree that this is something they were brought up to handle and thrive at. However, running domestic affairs as a young girl assisting her mother differs from when the weight of responsibilities lies solely on her as a wife. Where domestic help is available and desired, this can significantly assist in maintaining balance. At the same time, a man's place is not diminished by his joining in the domestic activities of his own home. Being hands-on also endears children to their fathers. Many children are observed to be very close to their mothers, which is often inspired by her willingness to relate with them in informal setups, doing simple activities that don't seem nerve-wracking. It is this informal communication that is depicted in *Deuteronomy 6:6-9. And these words that I command you today shall be on your heart. You shall teach them diligently to your children, and shall talk of them when you sit in your house, and when you walk by the way, and when you lie down, and when you rise. You shall bind them as a sign on your hand, and they shall be as frontlets between your eyes. You shall write them on the doorposts of your house and on your gates.*

2. **A Focus on Making Time Spent Together Enjoyable-** I think this would require that I appeal to your wise heart. All couples need time together to bond and understand each other. Hence, the need to work as a team without undue strife and hatred. What are you willing to give to experience this daily? Third-party (your relations, associates, and friends or his) must not be allowed to break your *'leaving and cleaving'* process. They have their own roles but

must not be allowed to cross the necessary boundaries.

3. **Sacrifice and Compromise:** Something sometimes must give way. Life demands sacrifices from everyone at some stage or the other. Therefore, you must hold the mindset that you might need to sacrifice or compromise some things that can be delayed to a later date or set aside totally in favor of a loving and peaceful home. Sometimes, the idea is a win-win. Some other times, win-loose is wisdom. I (Abigail) call it stooping to conquer. Yes, it is a book and a principle I have utilized in many challenging situations to preserve my home. We are doing great with more than five decades to our credit. Olubunmi initially disliked this principle, but thankfully, we witnessed its impact for many years.

4. **Openness and Accountability.** This idea may threaten an insecure person or where the spouse

has not shown good reasons to invest trust in them. However, an open person communicates that he has nothing to hide and is willing to be held accountable. I (Olubunmi) know that some men are often unwilling to practice this, especially with money and financial planning. It takes a secure man to humble his purse to the extent of his wife having a say in the expenses and investments. This I would leave to your level of growth and character. I can only admonish that if you want a well-coordinated home where no secrets and curveballs are coming your way, you need to consider being open and working at being accountable as a couple.

5. **A Non-competitive Atmosphere.** (Abigail speaking) More of complimenting rather than comparing. If you must always win, you must find a competitive sport to direct that energy towards. It is laudable to have such a drive, but it is draining for the spouse of an addicted

winner. Such a household is controlled by the ever-competing spouse who would inspire distrust and resentment over time. It is like a bomb waiting to explode. The willingness to collaborate and allow the other person to have a say is essential. No doubt, a woman is expected to submit by and large. Still, the man would want to be sure that his actions and manner of reaching decisions aren't later creating a bigger problem in the home. Do not assume that a non-resistant or non-vocal woman is in sync with you. Allow her voice her thoughts and listen from a non-judgmental standpoint. When people constantly compare themselves with others, it questions the worth of others. It also makes a spouse wonder whether their views are valuable, hence the risk of creating a tense environment. No team thrives in such a space.

6. **Celebrating Individuality:** Two different people are forming one united front in a family; as

such, a uniqueness exists already. However, the problem is that many people try to change their spouses to become like them or suppress their unique features. The way I (Olubunmi) see it, you can choose to imagine that each of you is bringing some exceptional value to the table. Imagine the man has forty strengths, and the wife has fifty-five. If they are all harnessed at different times, the home enjoys the dividends of such a setup. It might require an added mindset of selflessness and confidence in one's ability to comfortably honor and celebrate one's spouse. You realize there is no reason to compare and mourn when you don't have a specific strength. My husband and I (Olubunmi) are like (as we say in Nigeria) Coke and Fanta. No two people can be more different. We probably define the statement, "Opposites attract." We are so much in sync, and it can only be God's doing.

7. **Unity:** This is integral in team building. This must be dealt with if either spouse feels they

don't belong to the team for any reason. Sometimes, the team is fractured because of relatives and other family ties and demands. These must be addressed. No one can reasonably ask for teamwork if the family unit is not seen as one. The healthy thing is prioritizing the who and what comes first, second, etc.

Of course, the immediate family members should be made second to the family the couple is building. The extended family should be 3rd on the list of priorities. Imagine that a woman is asked to continue her studies because of the financial strain it would bring on the family. Then she finds out (by some stroke of luck) that her husband has been financing the education of some siblings of his to higher levels even beyond what she has attained. Such a woman would shrug at the idea of submitting, and teamwork would sound like an abuse in her ears. It will stink.

The secrecy will hurt. It will create distrust and a feeling of being toyed with or used. Not to forget that she will feel her husband did not prioritize her. Trust becomes broken, and unity will be overlooked too. It will be pretty challenging to rebuild.

8. **Unconditional Acceptance of Each Other:** The best of us is still human, meaning that we are all subject to frailty and don't have everything under control at all times. We might even give our best, but sometimes, one person's best is the other's average. So rather than tearing each other down, learning to accept each other while encouraging growth and improvement is essential. Did you call it tolerance? Yes, tolerance is necessary for a successful marriage.

9. **Unselfishness:** The human mind is self-focused on a good day. It would demand that you make a conscious effort to take the attention off yourself to foster a healthy relationship based on mutual respect, care, and consideration for each other.

10. **Keep the Big Picture in View:** The challenge in life is the ability to keep the prize in sight. Many people fight for the essential details, but these can be made into mountains that aren't easy to do away with. So, make a conscious effort to keep the image of the home you are building in mind. Describing what you want ensures you don't crush what you build due to temporary frustrations. In deep heart-to-heart conversations, you would need to trash the idea of your goals and aspirations to ensure you two are on the same page and painting the same work of art.

On the whole, these are my (Olubunmi's) two most priced suggestions regarding building a team in your marriage: First, you must realize that you are each coming to the table with special abilities, unique stories, and crucial strengths to support the family that you are both buildings. One party in a marriage often fails to see the strengths or values the other party is bringing. You can imagine a man telling himself that his wife is only helping through domestic affairs or just having babies. That sounds so disrespectful, but it is also very naïve.

Yes, each of you has weaknesses, and neither of you is perfect, but each of you has a wealth of abilities that can complement each other. When you appreciate each other's abilities, working on communicating is the next essential thing. The flow of information has to be smooth and open. No issue should be out of bounds within a healthy marriage. Talk, but of course, be mindful about the words you utter so that you don't hurt your spouse.

CHAPTER 7.

CULTURAL DEMANDS VERSUS SUBMISSION

The cultures we belong to cannot be separated from our lives. You might try to adjust to new behaviors, but cultures take time to form and change. Except you want to face the challenges of relating with people of a specific culture without their buy-in and approval, we often cave in and apply the cultural demands. Sometimes, where culture gets loud is with extended family members. They are the family your spouse loves, knew, and gathered support from before you came into the picture (male or female). Some, however, introduce or remind you of practices in force from time immemorial. The demands might be godly, honoring, or loving. Still, sadly, in some situations, they can be demeaning, hateful, stressful, and outrightly ungodly.

The first question that should run through your mind as a wife is, *"what is my husband saying here?"* If he is silent, you have a problem, especially if it is ungodly or illegal. The ideal situation would be for the husband to answer. Several times, I have jokingly asked that a question be directed at my husband. I know our decision on the matter would best be heard from my husband. Some things don't lie appropriately in the mouth of the wife (especially in some cultural settings).

I know the reasoning some might have is that you are equal, and you are the same. Yes, yes, yes, yes. These are true, but wisdom requires that you remember that extended families are still human and might not embrace the concept of oneness in marriage. While you and your spouse know you are both equal, you allow each person to play the role most suitable to achieve/maintain love, peace, and order. I have had a friend whose husband once asked her to answer his mother in a specific way. It wasn't rude, but a hard truth that her mother-in-law would have held against her for life. I was glad she spoke with me. She knew it wasn't a smart move, and her hesitation was golden. A woman of wisdom, she is, I must say. When her husband conveyed the same message, his Mum did not like it. She shrugged it off after several renewed comments about disliking the statement. Imagine if his wife made the statement; I can bet that, all hell would have been let loose.

It is also possible that relations come directly to you and mount pressure. If you knew a little about the family's culture beforehand, here is where you would be grateful that you did. You would have thought it through, prayed it through, and felt it through. Your answer must be wise, calm, and respectful. One of the prayers I often pray, especially when remembering my in-laws, is "Lord, don't let wisdom be scarce in my life." I am married into a Godly family, but the devil tries to harm Godly families from within. I have said no to many things. Some I acted without saying the word 'No,' and the party who could have been offended was merry with me the next minute.

Every woman needs to realize that the culture she marries into is of two parts, the general, which is applicable in that tribe mostly. Then there is that of the individual family. I (Olubunmi) would explain it this way. You can be a woman of the Cushite tribe of Kenya and choose to marry a Danish-speaking man from Germany. You would have a lot to learn: the general German culture, the general Danish culture, and the specific culture of his family of origin. It is kind of a life of constant learning for such a couple. I have realized that the mothers or matriarchs of the family determine the culture retained in the family. Aren't we glad that we are so powerful? Hence, everyone who wants to enjoy peace in their home must make it a duty to learn and adapt to the cultures they can afford to honor.

However, I also hope that couples realize that while they do not throw their families' cultures away, they stay aware that their family unit is distinct. Their family can create new traditions and negotiate through to have new cultures. Sometimes, cultures make draconian and abusive demands on women. I think that is where one must draw the line. The only problem with this is that the community you belong to would first frown at your refusal to comply, which might attract sanctions. Interpretations of what is abusive can be relative and subjective, so they can be challenging to defend.

Let me come in here. I (Abigail) advise you to apply wisdom. Some things can be rejected but wisely and without any disdain or disrespect. Also, learning about the cultural demands relating to as many social contexts as possible beforehand would be fantastic. There is a practice in two tribes of Nigeria and a Namibian tribe where a guest is honored by the host's wife by spending the night with the guest. Knowing beforehand that such a culture exists in your tribe or your husband's tribe, the husband can simply take his guest to a guest house or hotel. The wife does not need to say a word to the guest in defiance. If the husband refuses and wants to offer her to his guest, she must refuse gracefully and respectfully. Such an experience should tell her more about her husband's values. She would need to pray because any man who would honor culture or tradition above God's Word would destroy himself and others as he goes. Submission does not serve as a license to sin. Adultery is a sin, and even where the husband insists, the sin is still a sin.

Therefore, dear wife, your code of conduct with your in-laws is simple- ***walk in honor and love.***

CHAPTER 8.

THE GROANING OF A SUBMISSIVE WIFE

Submission has never been easy, so we decided to write this book to ease the strain of any family applying these principles. It, however, can be deeply troubling and even frustrating when submission is forced on a woman. I (Abigail) have captioned this: *the groaning of a submissive wife.* Just like childbirth, the desired outcome is thrilling and always a joy that she looks forward to, but it comes with its hardships and stresses. We want anyone who reads this book to see through the eyes of that woman you are screaming at should submit. Olubunmi and I have talked several times about how upsetting and stressful it is not to take charge or handle things in specific ways. Women often have ideas and solutions that might work, but then, the man of the house says-PAUSE, WAIT, NO, OR even YES TO SOMETHING YOU ARE UNPREPARED FOR. It may sound funny after the event has passed, but it can become a seed of bitterness if not well managed.

She asks herself: 'why?' 'Are my ideas that insignificant?' 'Am I meant to sacrifice all?' 'Is it really worth it?' 'Am I going to reap someday the excellent fruit I have sown?' 'How can I keep my sanity when he has the final say?' 'Should I keep things from him today and forge ahead my way and at my own pace?' 'Why should God want to suppress us women so much?' 'Doesn't He have feelings?' 'Must I pray about everything?' 'I thought God gave us a brain, so we don't bug Him?' 'Where are my ambitions in this picture?' 'Can I do this?'

Take it from an older woman. It is challenging, but it gets better because the more you yield to the Holy Spirit, the more you see Him gain ground in your family. Some of those beautiful stories you have admired in other marriages would have been aborted if the wife failed to submit. Do not make your husband your focus. He will annoy you many times, to be candid. Focus on what matters: your submission to God. Don't allow yourself to get frustrated or overwhelmed. Be mindful of those you speak to in your upset state. Some counselling would move in the direction of your pain or frustration. They might not be bad people but simply people who are easily emotionally swayed. You can survive speaking those vile words and allowing his method to sail through this time. If it fails, he knows you warned him and will listen far more intently next time. You have gained his respect. If you see him walking into danger, give your advice and pray. Like I say to people: report him to His Maker. You would be shocked how things get sorted out after a heartfelt session with God. Remember, God loves your husband far more than you do. Relying on God is not a sign of weakness but great wisdom and trust.

CHAPTER 9.

THE VOICE OF A SUBSERVIENT WIFE

You must find it funny that I (Olubunmi) write on this after discussing the submissive wife. I smile at myself, but I think it is wise because I am younger, and *'Maami'* might have forgotten some nasty thoughts. I hope you get the joke. Subservience means the woman is put under. She did not necessarily put herself under but has been made to sometimes surrender her will before realizing she has the right to grant it.

The scenario is often mistaken for submission. Sometimes, a woman who isn't being abused might think she is being forced or made subservient simply because she doesn't understand. Some women never heard "No" while growing up. They got all they wanted. They had their way and did what they pleased. So, getting married and one man born of a woman saying, "No, you can't go to that event," would sound oppressive, controlling, or even abusive. A subservient wife often never knew she could offer some value and reasoning. She tells herself her options are few, if any at all. She might not realize it, but her voice is lost, her self-esteem eroded, and her self-worth sounds like a mirage. She feels she is being noble or agreeable but doesn't realize they have failed to build a family they will one day be proud of. Her children grow up to either hate her, pity her, or be like either her or their dad.

The Father was the oppressor who had now raised behaviourally disturbed protégées like him who would someday dominate their spouses. She is a second-class citizen in her own home, and she is as good as a hired maid - she may be only a bit different because she serves her husband sex occasionally. She inspires fear because fear has been the ruling sceptre in her home. Life depresses her even where she smiles, but she knows her zest for life and unique abilities have been wasted. Her needs matter to no one. She feels miserable and hopes that someday it will miraculously turn out to be worth it. Sadly, somewhere in her heart, she knows the caging has done so much harm. She walks the earth in shame and pain. Over time, she feels used, toyed with, and outright dishonored. Where the scope and intent of submission are not godly, no one will enjoy a healthy marriage in such a setup. Where abuse or humiliation is used as a control measure, a wife needs to ask herself how she made this okay or acceptable.

The subservient wife finds 'joy' in her service to her family as though she is being assessed. A submissive wife knows her scorecard is God-issued, so she serves by drawing strength from God. The submissive wife loves to help her family but doesn't rely on them for her joy, as she derives this from God.

CHAPTER 10.

TOOLS FOR SUBMISSION

It would be a travesty to say all we have said and not discuss how to practically deliver on this life-long submission project. It requires your heart, mind, and body. Your tongue had better be on board. We both have had epic fails with our tongues, so believe me (Abigail) when I say you need it on board. Your tongue, after your heart, is the following tool that must yield to God's help. So, let's list your tools:

1. **Yielded-ness:** Here, the idea is to ensure one has an attitude that is not combative, controlling, domineering, or always competitive.

2. **Cultivate trust for your spouse:** I hope you marry a trustworthy person. It is difficult to trust a cheat, liar, or manipulative person. Do

yourself the service of choosing a person you can grow to trust.

3. **Humility:** You have heard us talk about this a lot in this book. Some people equate submission with humility, so you can understand how integral it is here. The idea is to ensure that you aren't haughty or arrogant.

4. **A Lifestyle of Prayer:** It is necessary to constantly grow in knowledge and the word of God. Endeavor to be relevant spiritually and intellectually.

5. **Adopt an Attitude of Service:** If you are too big to serve, then you are too big for submission and, by extension, too big for marriage. Service is leading less visibly. It is honorable and should never be seen as demeaning but given in love. Ask him once in a while, *"Do you need anything? Is there anything I can do for you? Can I help?"*

6. **Ensure Self-control is Your watchword:** You will be tempted to flip. Don't let your emotions run wild. You need to be in control by God's

grace at all times. Titus 2:5 encourages wives *'to live wisely and be pure, to work in their homes, to do good, and to be submissive to their husbands. Then they will not bring shame on the word of God.'* (NLT) Olubunmi jokes about praying incessantly for temperance every day because she is well aware of her temperaments. We all need it truly.

7. **Cultivate the Spirit of Amenability:** By this, I mean to be 'leadable.' Be soft, receptive, responsive, and agreeable. Check out *1 Peter 3:4-5 "But let your adorning be the hidden person of the heart with the imperishable beauty of a gentle and quiet spirit, which in God's sight is very precious. For this is how the holy women who hoped in God used to adorn themselves, by submitting to their own husbands." ESV*

8. **Negotiation:** A commanding tone might intimidate and be resisted, but one who can negotiate without manipulating is a strong and wise woman.

9. **Good Communication Skills:** It is often said that women expect men to know how they feel. However, this is practically impossible. Your views must be communicated verbally in a non-confrontational manner.

10. **A Willingness to Be Wrong:** There have been times when I (Olubunmi) wanted to be wrong. I had found that just that willingness offered a soft landing for both of us (my husband and I) when I was wrong. Sometimes, we so desperately want to be right that we work at it to say- *"You see that I was right all along."* This further strains the relationship, and men hardly open up afterward if they know they might be bashed for making mistakes. But I must confess that we both have a good laugh when either of us turns out to be wrong.

11. **Constant Willingness to Forgive.** Forgiveness is the gift you give your relationship so that a new chapter can start. A bitter heart is darkened and can be very tedious to relate to. The mere willingness to forgive makes several

offenses light and provides an atmosphere of acceptance.

Here are a few practical tips that might help:

1. **Have a good attitude towards your husband's decisions:** Do not go around the house sulking or grumbling when you "allow" him to make the final decision. If you are worried, calmly offer your advice and start to pray. You probably do not want your worries to be justified in the long run.

2. **Practice keeping quiet:** I (Olubunmi) am highly opinionated, vocal, a fast thinker, and a talker. I have found that just swallowing saliva can save the day. If the first thought that came to mind got on my lips, a war would have ensued in seconds. So, practice silence. When you have rephrased your statement, and it is seasoned with grace, then share it. It would do much more wonders than the yell you were about to unleash.

3. **Don't sweat the small stuff**: Avoid making a mountain from a molehill. I (Olubunmi) have learned to say to myself: *'Life is not this difficult, God dey.'* This means I won't trouble myself about all issues because God exists. Sometimes, it means making a potentially big issue look small psychologically to tackle it with fewer emotions.

4. **Don't be the savior of your marriage at all times**: I know that many of us women learned Abigail's story in the Bible (1 Samuel 25:2-42). And sometimes we live for such a dramatic experience. However, you may displace your husband by always taking the lead in solving the problem. You may kill his confidence to lead and spoil him so that he either becomes lazy (and frustrates you further) or resent you for emasculating him.

5. **Don't constantly question his decisions**: This speaks to the tone, situation, location, number of times, etc. Supposing you are the type of person who must always know why, you are

not too much of a good follower or trusting lover. For instance, if your husband asks you to wait at your office until he comes to pick you up, don't conclude that he is hiding something at home simply because it is not his usual practice. You may jump into the next available vehicle and, twenty minutes later, realize that you are at the center of an active fight between two warring groups and therefore get stranded. You may wonder why he didn't tell you this was his reason. Then he gets to your office and tells you his previous call was with the last few seconds of airtime on his mobile phone. He didn't think loading airtime to explain was as crucial as acting fast. He had heard about the blood bath in town and was rushing to get out of his office, pick up the kids from school, pick you up, and lodge you all in a hotel away from that route. Your husband might not always make the best heroic decisions, but learn to encourage him and allow him to lead.

6. **Ask God for grace and patience**: This is helpful, especially when you don't understand why. Patience never has a timetable issued to it. It might need renewal at times, so please ask God. He gives it generously.

7. **Be mindful of how you relay his decisions to others**: People can sense whether you agree with your husband on an issue. For some, it could raise concerns and make them worried about trusting you as a team, while for other ill-hearted people, they could begin to consider how to slide in and cause more rifts. If his decision is not ungodly or illegal, please defend it.

8. **Practice active listening**: You know how annoying it is to talk to someone who is not giving you their attention. Instead, they are doing something else or just ignoring you. When conversing, give him your attention. Yes, I know; he should do the same too.

9. **Transparent love must be practiced**: Try hard
to run away from self-righteousness that would
only make you cocky.

CHAPTER 11.

SUBMISSION WITHOUT

HEARTACHE

(OLUBUNMI AND ABIGAIL)

Learning to submit is a task no one masters overnight. We still falter, so don't beat yourself up. No one is perfect. One can do some things to prevent the undue strains that might come with submitting. The following pieces of advice would save you a lot of stress and psychological torture:

1. Marry a man who understands his role and has the maturity and humility to grow into playing his part for the rest of his life.

2. Marry a man with a teachable spirit.

3. Marry a man who loves, fears, and serves God.

4. Marry a man who is responsible to other men- mentors, pastors, godly friends.

5. Marry a man who loves and respects you- your views, your perspective in life, and even your relations.

6. Marry a man who is graceful and not controlling.

7. Marry a man who takes the initiative and is willing to use the leadership language: "Let us do so and so________." Many women struggle with men who don't lead but wait to be told they are in charge. Along the way, the woman jumps in the lead probably because she trusts her instincts, distrusts him, or is simply because she is an Alpha female, as it were. If your husband does not already display his leadership ability, you must inspire and nudge him towards the same. Boost his confidence that you are willing to follow and trust his sense of judgment while giving your input in a calm and non-attacking manner.

8. Marry a well-adjusted man: Socially awkward men might be great in spiritual things but often struggle with inner security challenges such as

self-esteem and self-worth. The competitive spirit or jealousy that cages a wife through her husband's rules often stems from his lack of faith in himself and his fear of being overshadowed. A secure mindset is priceless for both parties in a marriage.

9. Guard against the extremes of legalism and liberalism: Your home is not meant to be a militant religious platform, nor a platform for disorderliness anarchy. The extremes of legalism and liberalism bring spirits and attitudes that do not honor God. They are often products of a mind dependent on itself, its pride in its responsible lifestyle, and trust in its ability not to be accountable for its actions. The grace mindset says- I am human and have received such a great package of unconditional love. I can only show my gratitude by reciprocating God's love by loving others responsibly and respectfully.

10. Choose your spouse with God's guidance. Don't trust yourself alone to make this choice.

You need to ask your heavenly Father. He knows the end from the beginning. He knows the heart of man, hence the need to trust Him.

11. Humility: A humble person faces less combat and can make peace quickly. Besides, humility is excellent for negotiation, especially with a man. Arrogance puts most men off.

12. Self-control- If you aren't self-controlled, it is time to work at it. Being rash or unbridled is one of the worst things you can do to your marriage. Women who are always brash or act/talk recklessly or incessantly are likely to cause tension in their homes. Ensure you train yourself and receive the Holy Spirit's guidance while having a tongue full of grace.

13. Patience: Getting things your way or when you want them to happen can be a sure way to mount pressure on yourself and, eventually, on your marriage. Patience takes the heat off the emotional environment in your home such that a huge issue can become a molehill because it is not attacked with pressure and worry. Learn to

allow things to flow and fall where they may. If it is a vital issue, pray and let God take charge in His way and time.

14. Ability to negotiate wisely: Negotiation skills are vital tools. Many women do not know how to deal. They think negotiating means being manipulative and controlling things which is not the case. A negotiator realizes that one must consider a win-win situation in some situations. This means that you need to be ready to listen and understand what the other person wants, find a way to compromise or incorporate their desires and present a plan that works for both of you. If you must always win, you might lose much more than you bargained for in the long run.

15. Ability to forgive: You might wonder why we are adding this here. The truth is that your spouse might do some very hurtful, reckless, or self-centred things to you. They might be acting badly and still want you to consider them. While you work to get them to see

reason and improve, you would likely become bitter or vengeful if you harbor anger and resentment. I know that forgiveness is hard when offensive conduct is ongoing, but please ask God for help so that it does not become a vicious cycle of pain in your home. Forgive offenses and offenders, even perceived ones. You do yourself a more excellent service and favor by forgiving.

16. A deep and consistent prayer life: You cannot rely solely on the physical dimension we see. You and your spouse are spirit beings. The wise approach would be to involve God in all of your affairs. Pray daily. It's a secret tool to ensure your home is orderly and peaceful. Pray individually and as a family. A family that prays and communicates has a greater chance of staying together.

17. Do not cast off your confidence: A confident woman is a treasure, alluring and appealing. Be assured but not arrogant. The average man is put off by pride or a woman whose attitude is

on a high horse. Confidence says to the world-
"I deserve to be here, and I know how to maintain my lane and give my best. I know my worth and function boldly without fear of reproach because I intend to deliver daily."

18. Nurture honor and respect: These are tied to having a humble heart. Your culture may determine what is considered honorable many times. Find what suits your unique family setup and speak honor in words and comportment daily. It tells the man that you are offering it gladly and expecting the same in some way in return. Most men flee when they are treated in disdainful manners. It puts them off or makes them antagonize you—something you can avoid totally. I know a man who once fled a relationship because the woman was often disrespectful and dishonoring. You may also be aware of similar stories. The man isn't chauvinistic; he is just not accepting abuse. If your spouse feels put down, watch it and make the necessary adjustments.

19. Forgive yourself. We all have fallen short of this glorious marriage duty. Repent of your wrong ways. Ask for forgiveness where necessary and let it go. We both have had to do so several times in our individual lives. If you won't, your confidence is at stake.

20. Learn from women who are succeeding. *Titus 2:3-5[6] "Similarly, teach the older women to live in a way that honors God. They must not slander others or be heavy drinkers. Instead, they should teach others what is good. These older women must train the younger women to love their husbands and their children, to live wisely and be pure, to work in their homes, to do good, and to be submissive to their husbands. Then they will not bring shame on the word of God." (NLT)*

I know many women loathe the idea of mentorship by another woman. It is sad, though, because the Bible makes provision for older women to teach younger ones. Learn to

____

[6]Titus 2:3 NLT: Similarly, teach the older women to live in ....
https://biblehub.com/nlt/titus/2-3.htm

learn from others. Prayerfully ask God's leading to know whom to learn from. Your marriage must be protected from attacks, so don't blindly choose a mentor. You can also learn at seminars, talks, and fellowship meetings. Mentor others, especially your children (biological and otherwise). You are building the nation and preparing people for God's Kingdom.

You might ask: "What if I am already married, and my husband is far from ideal?" Our candid opinion is that you trust and pray a. that God throws His searchlight on you and show you who indeed you are, b. that God changes you if need be so that your home is His Kingdom on earth, c. that God helps your husband be who He wants Him to be. We can assure you that God would do the needful since you want to glorify Him. Seeking good marital counselling may also go a long way as you both desire to glorify God.

CHAPTER 12.

<u>WHO NEVER TO SUBMIT TO</u>

I (Abigail) know that some people who read this book are already in painful marriages. Your trauma is real, and many things discussed here sound like medicine after death or a further push down the subservient lane. As I write this, I am in my 70s, so I have had my share of challenges. I have also heard and seen a lot in the lives of people I have counselled. I would never advise anyone to submit to pain, especially if it is violent.

Many years ago, the general societal reasoning was that a woman should stay in her matrimonial home, irrespective of what was happening. I, sadly, saw women die through violence orchestrated by their husbands, which could have been averted. Many, though alive, are the living dead. They are enduring rather than enjoying their marriage.

The solution would have begun with the proper mindset about submission. Many women in abusive marriages are caged by the submission requirement. Another cage is the children's blackmail. If a spouse (male or female) sees evil and knows their life is in danger, preserving that life becomes the priority over and above the marriage. To some, dying in an abusive marriage is honorable. I beg to disagree. If your spouse threatens your life or acts in ways that could kill you or any child, please reach out. Don't blame it on submission.

God wants you to survive and thrive. There are ways to remedy some situations; seek professional counselling and therapy. But you first must be safe and alive. If a period of separation has to be endured, please allow the process. Before this period ends, you must also be confident that the abuser has repented. He must show that he understands the consequences, has gotten professional help, cares about you sufficiently, and is now accountable to other people besides themselves. Many abusive spouses are never responsible to anyone else. Unfortunately, you know you are at risk when married to a man or woman with no one to speak to or caution them when they misbehave. If you are in such a situation, it is time to pray regarding God humbling your spouse's heart and making them subject to godly authority. God would bring people their way, inspiring them to be better, more loving, teachable, and humble. Never isolate yourself. Otherwise, people who can help will not know what to do when challenges come.

While this list does not inspire you to rush for a separation or a divorce, it would be wise to pay attention to the abuse you might be suffering at the hands of the following people. These people need professional psychological help; therefore, you cannot assume you are safe with them simply because they are your wife or husband.

1. **Misogynists** are people who abhor, dislike, hate, despise, or are strongly prejudiced against women. You might wonder why you didn't

notice this during courtship or why you got married in the first place. Some people rush their courtship, so they don't allow time to reveal things. Some marry because they are of age, and their families are mounting pressure on them. Some men may not realize they hate women or may not want to admit that they have a weird mindset.

If you are married to one, ensure that you take his behavior before God in prayers and try to protect yourself as wisely as possible. Guard your heart because their words and behaviors would sometimes hurt. While forgiving is critical, don't be naïve by always opening yourself to pain. Knowing their frame of mind requires studying how to live above the pain and thrive in such a situation. Don't be shocked if, to spite you, he holds back on affection, love, compliments, encouragement, etc. If he devalues you, work at boosting your self-confidence. While not attacking him verbally or physically, uplift yourself consciously, such as with a list of positive affirmations.

This can be a very toxic environment, so I understand it would take a lot of resilience to remain in such a marriage. If someday you can convince him to enrol in professional counselling, it would sure do you good. This is not an ideal marriage situation; I understand your pain. If you can allow God's grace to pull you through, there is hope for a happy ending. However, if he gets violent, I would be the first to scream that you need to get out, even if it is for a season.

2. **Narcissists:** People with this disorder can have an exaggerated sense of self-importance and entitlement and require constant and excessive admiration. They expect to be recognized as superior, even without achievements that warrant it[7]. They crave worship, even if they

____

[7] President Trump Is In An Angry and Unstable State of Mind ....
https://wallstreetrebel.com/wsr/articles/president_trump_is_in_an_angry_a
nd_unstable_state_of_mind/2020-05-21-16-20-48.html

never agree that they do. For some reason, they exaggerate achievements and talents; they are preoccupied with fantasies about success, power, brilliance, beauty, or the perfect mate. They believe they are superior and can only associate with equally special people. They monopolize conversations and belittle or look down on people they perceive as inferior.[8]

Narcissists expect special favors and unquestioning compliance with their expectations as though they own you. They have an entitled mindset and boast about it. They take advantage of others to get what they want.[9] They have an inability or unwillingness to recognize the needs and feelings of others. They are secretly envious of others and believe that others envy them. They behave arrogantly or haughtily, boastful, and pretentious.

---

[8]Narcissism - Stop the Stigma. https://stopthestigma.org/narcissism/
[9] Understanding What a Narcissist Is - PairedLife.
https://pairedlife.com/problems/Mr-Perfect-turned-into-my-nightmare-that-never-ends-narcissistic-love

They would insist on having the best of everything. They are hardly violent but take cover if they ever get violent on you. Your first priority should be your safety. Don't bother about being right or explaining your side of the story; get out of harm's way first. They hardly forgive, are low on self-control, and can hardly treat people well. They talk down to anyone they deem less than them (including you). If they get violent, get to safety. After getting to safety, contact law enforcement and insist on counseling before any form of reconciliation requiring you to return to the same roof with the narcissist. Your life might be at risk.

If you are married to a person with this disorder, the first thing to do is nurture a healthy self-esteem. Your values form part of your identity and must never be eroded: guard them jealously. Wisdom is crucial to thriving in marriage, but always watch out that you don't submit to illegality or evil. Narcissists can do anything to achieve what they want. If they have marked you as a victim (not an equal or spouse to be respected), you could be sacrificed at any point. Realize that they hardly ever change and would play emotional games on you; hence the need to be emotionally and mentally resilient. If the person submits their hearts to God (not just a religious accent), they can change, but outside of that, do not weave your life around their antics.

3. **Violent men or women:** If a slap occurs once, you need to take a stand to stop further violence because it usually escalates over time. One slap becomes two, then becomes a kick, a punch, burns, and hospital visits. Condoning abuse of any kind is not Biblical submission, especially if it is violent.

The list can be longer, but I imagine you understand the warning. Submission is vital for a healthy home, but apply wisdom and be strategic where there is danger.

CHAPTER 13.

<u>HOW TO KNOW YOU AREN'T SUBMITTING</u>

For me (Olubunmi), submission is one of those things that I identify more in my life when I am defaulting. I sense something is wrong when I am critical, impatient, defiant, or snap at him. Or when I rush in and take control, take charge, or get irritated at his "slow pace." And even when I fail to allow my husband the opportunity to be a man and provide godly headship for our family, I know I need a heart check. These might sound familiar:

- You hate the concept of submission. Be true to your heart. There is no way you would hate a thing and then embrace or utilize it.

- Your husband doesn't feel respected. Your attitude is speaking.

- You are constantly correcting your husband.

- You are the decision-maker in your marriage.

- Your children consistently come to you after your husband decides, and you don't honor your husband's decision.

- Your husband has withdrawn emotionally.

- You discuss every disagreement you have with your husband with others to vindicate yourself. You want to ensure you make him sound wrong while you are right. It is like you need a following to reinforce your viewpoint. You are looking for worldly validation.

- You are stubborn about accepting correction. You hate being corrected, so the behaviors that upset your marriage continue.

- You embrace a feminist movement mindset, even in marriage. Note that feminism <u>as a concept</u> is not harmful, but how it has been perceived and taught over the years as a weapon of attack against men is where the problem lies. If, as a believer in feminism, you fail to realize the command structure in your home, you will destroy your home from within over time. Yes, you are equal, even as the Bible says, but you are wise enough to understand that order requires structure.

CHAPTER 14.

WHEN SUBMISSION FAILS YOU.

This is the most challenging chapter to write. We must admit that sometimes, women submit, and their stories make us question why they ever did. Imagine a woman who submits her income and later finds out that her husband used it to finance his side chick. When the wife accosts him in her heartbroken state, he boasts that all she owns is his. He even quotes the scripture that says her body is his and tells her he will move in with his mistress. I imagine you are asking why she made her money available to him? (Actually, in a healthy marriage, nothing should be hidden. A wife should have 100% access to her husband's funds and vice versa).

In the case described above, the husband took advantage of her forthrightness. In situations where trust has been eroded, it is tough to regain. Stories like this have been familiar lately, hence a global distrust for submission and openness in marriage.

While we hope that more men learn to live the Christ-like way, what should the woman do? She is hurt, and rightly so. The list of accusations is long, bringing with it all kinds of emotions. I have counselled a few women in this situation, and the first thing I say regarding the money is that she should not accept the devil's lie that she was stupid. She was and still is a godly woman. Her assessor is God, and He sees that she was good to her husband and knows who needs some *'spanking.'* It indeed isn't she that needs the *'spanking.'*

Next is to spend some valuable time with God in a heart-to-heart conversation. It is now for her to heal and control what is left of her precious life and resources. Most cheating husbands realize they are wrong. While some never return to acknowledge that they were wrong, the wife should be comforted that

God (her actual assessor) is proud of her and sees her pains. She, of course, will be justified in denying her husband further access to her money. God alone can restore all she has lost and make her whole again.

When the chips are down, the side chicks and others evaporate into the air. It's the man and his wife that are left to face life. A wife must decide whether to forgive him and allow God to heal her or if she would rather walk away and leave the marriage. The foolishness of a cheating spouse can significantly harm a home, sometimes to irreparable extents. So, I would not decide for any one but expect that each person in such situation spend some quality time with God making crucial decisions they will have to live with for the rest of their lives.

CHAPTER 15.

<u>TO OUR MEN- HUSBANDS, AND HUSBANDS-TO-BE.</u>

You know what? Our daughters and sisters will be cross with us if we don't speak to you in this book. This is also to prevent some of you who would gloat with this book in the face of your wives.

Okay, jokes apart, what are the responsibilities of the husband of a submissive wife? This will be brief, as we know that men are often of few words.

If one were to write a book on this, it wouldn't be out of place. We won't speak in detail on this here. However, a few questions are essential:

1. How well do you love and honor God?
2. How do you see your life in your 50s, 60s, 70s, or 80s?
3. What value do you place on your wife?

4. Do you intend to have a vibrant and healthy marriage?

5. What examples do you want your children to imbibe?

6. Would you like your daughters to be treated the way your wife is currently treated by you and your side of the family?

7. What do you honor more? Your pride or your home?

To be candid, your responsibility can be summarized by this statement – **MAKE LIFE EASY FOR YOUR WIFE**. It's a two-way thing. Her assignments are to buffer you, protect you, support you, promote you, assist you, honor you, and believe in you. The list is endless- Proverbs 31:10-31. Yours are to make the environment conducive for her to accomplish these and more.

We are all human; hence, we all have things that irritate, frustrate, annoy, or even depress us. Emotions are as real as they get, and expectations never seem to die, so what should you do?

1. **Submit to God:** Kindly start as we did by submitting to God. If you don't submit to God, you are already a source of heartache because you would go out of line simply by default and won't be the only victim of the consequences. Some repercussions are so grave that the children in the next few generations may suffer. Consider King Saul, who was impatient about sacrificing to God. If only he had submitted to God's instructions, his lineage would have remained on the throne forever *1 Samuel 10:8, 1 Samuel 13:8-14*. He showed that he wasn't going to submit to God by waiting for Samuel. There would never have been a need for David.

2. **Embrace Loving Your Wife:** It is sometimes crazy hard, but it's a vital foundation for your home and your wife's emotional safety. If loving a complicated woman is hard, still love her

because you might have a winning chance. Love does so many things:

- Love helps you to grow.
- Love protects families
- Love forgives
- Love dispels fear
- Love conquers hate
- Love inspires confidence in the recipient

The Bible's instructions are clear. Christ loves the Church in the same manner. Hence, asking you to love her does not demean you or cause you to lose your position as head of the family. Loving her uplifts you. It sets you in proper standing before God and men of honor.

Ephesians 5:25-29 reads, *"Husbands, love your wives just as Christ loved the church and gave his life for it. He did this to dedicate the church to God by his word, after making it clean by washing it in water, to present the church to himself in all its beauty—pure and faultless, without spot or wrinkle or any other imperfection. Men ought to love their wives just as they love their own bodies. A man who loves his wife loves himself. ([10]None of us ever hate our own bodies. Instead, we feed and take care of them, just as Christ does the church, for we are members of his body.) As the scripture says, "For this reason, a man will leave his father and mother and unite with his wife, and the two will become one."* (GNT) *This scripture reveals a profound truth, which I understand applies to Christ and the church.*

"Husbands, love your wives and do not be harsh with them." (Colossians 3:19, GNT)

3. **Lead as Jesus Did**: Studying the life of Jesus is not out of place. He led the disciples wisely and gracefully; service and love were His trademarks. He was

---

[10]Ephesians 5:29 Indeed, no one ever hated his own body, but ....
https://biblehub.com/ephesians/5-29.htm

their master but never lorded it over them. He was a God-like authority on earth, always honorable and worthy of respect. No, we don't expect perfection from you, but we hope you release yourself to God and try to conform to His image as we also try to. (II Corinthians 3:18, Romans 8:29, Galatians 5:225.)

5. **Nourish her-** *'None of us ever hate our own bodies. Instead, we feed them, and take care of them, just as Christ does the church, for we are members of his body.' (Ephesians 5:29, GNT).* It is your duty and an honorable man to nourish her. Imagine a malnourished person: he looks frail, sick, needy, and even close to death. Then, imagine that the woman you called your wife was malnourished. You might wonder what you will use to nourish, feed, or care for her? Please be creative, but always ensure that love and respect are at the root. Spending money on family members, especially your wife, is excellent. However, you

must be generous with kind words that honor and affirm her. Please pay attention to her, speak, and listen to her. Be her confidant and not her assessor. Of course, no one expects you to show love without correcting where she is wrong. Correcting in love is essential; otherwise, you wound her.

6. **Submit:** Next on this crucial list is learning to submit to your wife. Are you screaming, frowning, or cursing at me? This is where I wish I had asked '*Maami*' to write this. You sure won't do any of those at a woman in her 70s. I hope you are smiling now? You have the final say at home; you have the deciding vote; you give the orders, and your authority is not in a contest.

   However, being submissive to one another is still the Bible's admonition - ***Ephesians 5:21*[11]** *Submit yourselves to one another because of your*

---

[11]Ephesians 5:21 Submit to one another out of reverence for ....
https://biblehub.com/ephesians/5-21.htm

reverence for Christ. When this verse was written, it was not strictly for couples. However, if there is wisdom anywhere in the Bible that could do your marriage some good, wouldn't you take it? Submitting one to another means being considerate of one another. If the decision you are about to make can be discussed before taking action, wouldn't you do that to get her perspective? You still have the final say. However, this way, your wife does not feel taken for granted, dominated, inferior, or hurt.

For instance, you are new in a city and find out that the best schools are about an hour's drive from where you live. You want your children to attend one of such schools. It would be wise to ask for your wife's opinion. You know that the nature of your job wouldn't allow you to do the school runs every morning and afternoon. Your children are young, so your wife needs to wake up as early as 4 am each day to prepare them and set out by 6 am if they won't be caught in traffic. No matter how submissive a woman is, which woman would thank you for putting her through such a stressful routine?

Do you remember the story of Abraham and Sarah, where Sarah asked that Haggar be sent away? God approved this request, which meant Abraham submitted it to Sarah. See *Genesis 21: 10-12.* In some situations, God expects that you listen to your wife and submit to her desires. May God give you wisdom daily.

7. **Be Respectful:** Lastly, ensure you are respectful and never domineering, especially when your blood relations are involved. I know these words- 'dominate and respect' could be relative in different contexts. Dominance is controlling irrespective of the desires or interests of the other. It is self-centered and can be wicked. Choose to be mild-mannered, though confident and assertive. Over time, dominance and disrespect would yield pain, hate, fear, and chaos.

In the same way, your husbands must live with your wives with the proper understanding that they are more delicate than you. Treat them with respect, because they also will receive, together with you, God's gift of life. Do this so that nothing will interfere with your prayers. (1Peter 3:7, GNT)

Didn't God make you one body and spirit with her? What was his purpose in this? It was that you should have children who are indeed God's people. So make sure that none of you breaks his promise to his wife. (Malachi 2:15, GNT)

A final word on this would be to remind you that your stance will affect your home, name, lineage, dynasty, legacies, life, wife, and children. **<u>THESE ARE ALL YOURS.</u>** Why not accept her as your teammate?

Ecclesiastes 4:9[12] *Two are better off than one because together they can work more effectively. If one of them falls down, the other can help him up. But if*

---

[12] Daily Bible Reading - September 25th, 2021 | American ....
https://americanbible.org/resources/daily-bible-reading?date=09-25-2021s

someone is alone and falls, it's just too bad, because there is no one to help him. If it is cold, two can sleep together and stay warm, but how can you keep warm by yourself? Two people can resist an attack that would defeat one person alone. A rope made of three cords is hard to break.

CHAPTER 16.

FACING CONFRONTATION AND THE CRITICS

There are bound to be criticisms and confrontations from many quarters on the submission issue. Your spouse may not even appreciate you, let alone other relations. 'Cowardly', 'oppressed', or 'fearful' are some names you should be ready to receive. Some people will think you are crazy for submitting to a man. Some will mock or scold you for not living the *"liberated life."* You might hear comments like, *"In this 21st century, a woman still defers to her so-called husband?" "Isn't she educated? Hasn't she heard of women's rights and affirmative action?" "I am a feminist, so I should not be expected to submit myself to any man. I bow my will to God alone." "I am an independent woman, I submit to no man, we are equals and partners. Afterall, I make more money than he does".*

The comments can be hunting and daunting. Let's help one another put things in perspective: ***NOWHERE IN OUR HEARTS OR THIS BOOK DO WE CONDONE EVIL, VIOLENCE, OR OPPRESSION OF WIVES. NO,*** *and a million times* **NO.** God does not condone it, and we will never do so. The problem, most times, stems from the fact that some things people call oppression these days are not oppression in the real sense. How is waiting to discuss with your husband a decision regarding your job oppressive? If you take a position that affects your family life, health, location, and so on without your husband's consent, you risk hurting YOUR home. Why not get his buy-in and then implement things to make it work smoothly too?

What should you do? How do you answer your critics and mockers? It may be difficult, as some attacks may come from close associates. Nevertheless, God's wisdom is available to help us navigate.

"It is not an enemy who taunts me. I could bear that. It is not my foes who so arrogantly insult me—I could have hidden from them. Instead, it is you—my equal, My companion and close friend. What good fellowship we once enjoyed as we walked together to the house of God". (Psalm 55: 12-14[13], NLT)

"Discretion is a life-giving fountain to those who possess it, but discipline is wasted on fools." (Psalm 16:22[14], NLT)

The following suggestions would prove helpful:

1. **Prayer makes a difference.** Remember, escapism is not the way out; overcome evil with good. Be prayerful and loving; ready to let go of the past. In her book "The power of a Praying Wife," Omartian Stormie urges us to pray that the Lord changes us(me) instead of asking God to change our spouse.

---

[13] Psalm 55:12 For it is not an enemy who insults me; that I ....
https://biblehub.com/psalms/55-12.htm
[14] Proverbs 16:22-24 NLT - Discretion is a life-giving ....
https://www.biblegateway.com/passage/?search=Proverbs+16:22-24&version=NLT

2. **Be resolute and focused.** Do you know why you are to submit? We believe the Holy Spirit has told you a lot if you have been reading this book up to this point. If your reasons for submitting are based on fear, you will most likely fail. The mockers will tear you into shreds. It would help if you fully understood why. If your love for God enabled you to submit to Him is the origin, then you started well. If you love your husband and are not competing with him, dear sister, you win. Finally, if you can add that you appreciate or envision what God intends to build through your home, then you are the reigning queen girl. *"Listen to Me, you who know what is right, you people with My law in your hearts: Do not fear the scorn of men; do not be broken by their insults."* (Isaiah 51:7, BSB)

3. **Trust and believe.** All relationships require trust, and it grows into a dynamic relationship. Speak the truth in love. Your fear about that issue may be merely a mirage. Do not jump to

hasty conclusions. You are a transformation agent. Do your best to impact your generation and future generations through your family in the church and the larger society. Beyond the conversion of the heart, aim to transform society. Remember this in your children's training and the relationship between you and your spouse's relations. In some communities, the woman/wife is simply a property (sad and inappropriate). Still, you can change the narrative with wisdom. Do you know that you can make a difference beginning with your family? You can change the history of your own nuclear family. There you have ample space to mold the correct values.

4. **Don't let the pains you have suffered sow seeds of vengeance.** Some innocent young women in the next generation might suffer at your hands if you do not prevent a reoccurrence of the pains that you have suffered. If you heal and deal with the pains, you can improve the quality of life your daughters-in-law will enjoy.

I (Abigail) have had the privilege of changing the climate in my home (all glory to God). I promised God many years before my first son got married that no young woman would face any of the pains and humiliation I faced due to Yoruba culture. I sat Olubunmi down, and I got her buy-in. You know that we women are the custodians of our family cultures. Oh yes, you might want to ask any of the four daughters-in-law that God gave me. If they say otherwise, I would like to know (my fingers are crossed with smiles).

So how did these changes occur? ___If you love your biological children, transfer the same affection to their spouses-male or female___. What if they don't reciprocate? You may be thinking. Don't worry. My mother-in-law of blessed memory (Madam Rachael Ayisat Oyinlola Olayemi), in one of her two most important prayers, would say: "Iwo na a se Iya oko." This means that "You too will become a mother-in-law." It is a powerful prayer that says: "You will reap what you sow." They will reap whatever they sow. Relax. Yours is to love them (your daughters/sons-in-law) as much as you love your biological children.

5. **Associate with people that have credibility and integrity**. This includes people with generational views who work to make a difference. We all need support. Let's be candid; being submissive is tough and can challenge your flesh and personality. We all need to hear a word of encouragement once in a while. Seek it out. Books like this will do you good. Read them again and again.

6. **Do not shout at your spouse, especially when the children (biological and otherwise) are present.** He might frustrate you. Remember that you are both human. Your husband is not perfect nor always prim or proper. The impact of shouting at him could create several ripple effects. If he is shy, you will hurt his confidence further, making him a less excellent leader. Breaking news- you would have just

shot yourself in the leg. If he is the bold type, you might get a reaction surpassing your reckless behavior, and you may not be happy afterward. Such men instinctively try to gain their headship position fast and sometimes at any cost.

7. **Be wise.** Don't let the devil capitalize on either of your weaknesses. **"Sensible people control their temper; they earn respect by overlooking wrongs."** (Proverbs 19:11, NLT)

"Avoiding a fight is a mark of honor; only fools insist on quarreling." (Proverbs. 20:3, NLT).

Don't hurt or insult your spouse, no matter the level of provocation, even when from his relations. I know this can be tough, but please resist the temptation. You might need to regulate time and access to you if their behaviors are poor towards you. You must, however, not become insecure, which will create other complications. An insecure woman is a walking timebomb. You don't want to be that anytime soon, trust us. Do not cast off your confidence. It is crucial for healthy living, especially if you must be around people who dislike or maltreat you. If you have been insulting, do not brush it off. Apologize profusely and please mean it. We have found that a heart-felt apology that may have felt too humbling actually would register in the mind of the one giving it as a means to most likely not repeat the same offensive action.

8. **Patience.** Patience is a virtue: pursue and pray for it, but be assertive against abuse. Forgive quickly: this is essential for your spiritual and physical health. *"Instead, be kind to each other, tender-hearted, forgiving one another, just as God through Christ has forgiven you." (Ephesians 4:32, NLT)*

9. **Daily soak yourself in the Word of God.** God's Word does a lot for our minds. It encourages, corrects, guides, and comforts. It is therapeutic, and gives calmness and serenity. Dear sisters, feast on it. I dare to say that it also keeps us sane. Some situations can almost run one crazy

if one isn't mindful, therefore saturate your mind with the Word. You will be glad you did. *"All Scripture is God-breathed and is useful for instruction, for conviction, for correction, and for training in righteousness, so that the man of God may be complete, fully equipped for every good work."* (2 Timothy 3:16-17, ESV) Meditation on the Word can keep your mind at peace. *"And now, dear brothers and sisters, one final thing. Fix your thoughts on what is true, and honorable, and right, and pure, and lovely, and admirable. Think about things that are excellent and worthy of praise".* (Philippians 4:8, NLT)

10. **Be determined to make the marriage work.** One of my (Abigail's) many stands is as simple as: "this marriage must work; it must glorify God." Diligently work on it. Marriage is work, honest hard work. Are you willing to do the work? Submission is paramount among the ingredients of success. Daily ask God to make you a solution and not a problem to humanity through your marriage.

CONCLUSION

We don't have much to say in conclusion. Know who you are in Jesus Christ. Let your identity sink in and be your confidence. It is not pride. Build up your relationship in and with God above all else. Don't be distracted by the negative comments you have proven wrong by dealing with them with the Word of God and on your knees. Know this- you are unique and carry out special duties in your marriage. What God is up to would gladden your heart and bless many. Amen!

PRAY WITH US:

Sometimes, our will is to do God's will, but we need help. Other times, when our will does not align with His, the battle becomes worse. Either way, prayer helps us submit to God and allows His Holy Spirit to access our hearts and minds. As a result, we become more like Jesus and accept His ways. Kindly join us in praying the following:

i.   Father God, help me to surrender to You and the Holy Spirit who lives in me.

ii.   Lord, help me to find a man who is submitted to you. Guide me and matchmake us. (If you are not yet married)

iii. Lord, help me to trust your Spirit's guidance in my marriage.

iv.   Lord, touch my husband and make him love and honor me.

v.   Lord, help me love and honor those dear to my husband (his mentors, family, and colleagues).

vi.   Lord, break me and mold me after the image of Jesus.

vii. Lord, give me counselors who will share wisdom at every stage of my journey in marriage.

viii. Lord, fill me with Your wisdom.

ix.   Lord, please help me deal with all my weaknesses and shortcomings.

x.   Lord, please help my husband deal with all his weaknesses and shortcomings.

xi.   Lord, forgive me of any rebellion in my heart.

xii.   Lord, please help me forgive myself for failing to live up to Your glory.

xiii.   Lord, breathe upon my marriage, heal all wounds, and make us fully yielded to Your supremacy.

xiv.   Lord, help my husband, and I realize our life assignments and live them passionately to Your glory.

xv.   Please teach me to walk in love and allow Your wisdom to rule me daily.

xvi.   Lord, please restrain evil counselors and influencers from hurting our home.

xvii.   Make my husband and me pillars in Your household, and may we inspire others to nurture their marriages.

xviii.   Lord, please guide our seeds so they will love godly marriages and not make poor choices.

xix.   Lord, please bless our children's spouses. Help them love and honor us. Let them be faithful helpers suitable for the life assignments You designed for each family unit.

xx.   Lord, breathe upon marriages in the world and let divorce and separation come to an end.

xxi. Lord, help ailing marriages in the body of Christ to heal and stand firm.

PROF JULIUS YINKA OLAYEMI AND DR. MRS ABIGAIL EBUN OLAYEMI

OLUBUNMI, DADDY, MUMMY, AND ADEWOLE

OLUBUNMI AND
ADEWOLE

<u>**ABOUT US:**</u>

Dr (Mrs) Abigail Ebun Olayemi is a mother of four sons and one daughter, mother-in-law to four lovely women and one meek young man. She is also a grandmother, sister, mentor, and wife to Prof Julius Yinka Olayemi. They got married on the 18th of December, 1971.

She has a Ph.D. in English and loves to write, cook and teach. She has taught Sunday school in her local Church, ECWA Chapel, Ilorin, for many years. She also served in the leadership of the Women's Fellowship of ECWA for many years. She is a member of the Board of Trustees of Phoebe's Nurturing Heart Foundation.

She has authored many devotionals and enjoys mentoring young women. Olubunmi calls her dad's armor-bearer and finds the concept of submission most visible in her, hence the book's inspiration. She lives in Ilorin, Kwara State, Nigeria.

Barrister Olubunmi A. Adewole-Babatunde is a Lawyer by training and a Life Coach by calling. She is a certified life coach (Secular and Christian). She has authored two other books - 'How to Fulfil Your Unique Life Purpose' and 'Life Syllabus.' She runs two Youtube Channels: Olubunmi Adewole-Babatunde and The Leadership Tv.

On August 24th, 2013, she married Dr. Adewole Babatunde, A man who has helped her be her best self. They live in Abuja, Nigeria.